MW00787379

Management for Professionals

More information about this series at http://www.springer.com/series/10101

Gilad Issar • Liat Ramati Navon

Operational Excellence

A Concise Guide to Basic Concepts and Their Application

Gilad Issar
Gedera
Israel

Liat Ramati Navon
Ness Ziona
Israel

ISSN 2192-8096   ISSN 2192-810X   (electronic)
Management for Professionals
ISBN 978-3-319-20698-1   ISBN 978-3-319-20699-8   (eBook)
DOI 10.1007/978-3-319-20699-8

Library of Congress Control Number: 2015957952

Springer Cham Heidelberg New York Dordrecht London
© Springer International Publishing Switzerland 2016
This work is subject to copyright. All rights are reserved by the Publisher, whether the whole or part of
the material is concerned, specifically the rights of translation, reprinting, reuse of illustrations,
recitation, broadcasting, reproduction on microfilms or in any other physical way, and transmission
or information storage and retrieval, electronic adaptation, computer software, or by similar or
dissimilar methodology now known or hereafter developed.
The use of general descriptive names, registered names, trademarks, service marks, etc. in this
publication does not imply, even in the absence of a specific statement, that such names are exempt
from the relevant protective laws and regulations and therefore free for general use.
The publisher, the authors and the editors are safe to assume that the advice and information in this
book are believed to be true and accurate at the date of publication. Neither the publisher nor the
authors or the editors give a warranty, express or implied, with respect to the material contained
herein or for any errors or omissions that may have been made.

Printed on acid-free paper

Springer International Publishing AG Switzerland is part of Springer Science+Business Media
(www.springer.com)

To my dear wife Tamar Gilad

Contents

Introduction

1

Recently, Operational Excellence has become a common term in discussions as well as an objective for P&L and performances improvement in industrial companies.

What are the latest industry dynamics and trends causing the rise in the importance of operational excellence?

Finance and the company P&L clearly call for gross margin improvements in the operation. Continuous improvement of the gross margin becomes a critical necessity in the current global economy. Since gross margin determines the product's pricing, improving it immediately increases the product's competitiveness in the market. Furthermore, since the operations teams control's around 50 % of the company's revenue spending they are responsible for the gross margin line in the company P&L. Operations can improve the company's bottom line results through continuous cost reduction.

Another trend, which has become significant during the last decade, is diversity and a worldwide spread of the product's production and supply chain. This global trend builds expectation for improvements in the supply chain's costs.

Furthermore, worldwide competition has become more agile and the time it takes a product to reach the market is constantly getting shorter. As a result, product's and technology's life spans are significantly shorter than they were in the past. From the management's and the company's financial stockholders point of view, a partial answer to the global trends, described above, is reaching operational excellence and shortening the time lines.

Within the operation's parameters, in yields, supply chains and in production costs, which are mostly controlled by the operations, the company's financial results can improve from moderate or good to excellent. There are many company success stories which prove that improvements in operations impact the company's P&L. Cases of turnarounds in P&L, from loss to profit, due to operational improvements are quite common.

How can we improve an operations performance from good or moderate to excellent?

© Springer International Publishing Switzerland 2016
G. Issar, L.R. Navon, *Operational Excellence*, Management for Professionals,
DOI 10.1007/978-3-319-20699-8_1

There are many theories and answers which come from diverse experience and from different schools.

*The theme of this book is, that simple, clear, professional, and **LEAN** operational rules, drive operations to **Operational Excellence**.*

Driving industrial companies to significantly improve in their P&L, through **Operational Excellence**, creates the following chain of financials benefits:

- Operational excellence increases the company's gross margin, which causes
- Cash to flow through to the company's bottom line, which brings
- Profit, which allows investments in the development of new products, which conquers customer trust and improves competitiveness in the market.

From the operation's and employee's aspect an Operational Excellence culture yields:

Lean and cost effective production,
A safe, high quality and technology leading operation
Empowered, motivated and innovative teams.

However as part of the business community, our paradigms and perceptions act as common obstacles that cause bias and prevent us from learning and applying changes which promote operational excellence. Firstly there is a rejection is to the change itself, which involves our known and predicted routine. Many times managers will not initiate improvement changes, even when financial results deteriorate, until an external factor is involved. Secondly, our perceptions on operational excellence, which are rooted in our financial, human resource, technology or industrial engineering backgrounds, will usually prevent us from adopting operational solutions, we will prefer ones that are in our area of expertise. The same company performance can be viewed through different perceptions depending on which different discipline, of the ones mentioned above, the analysts comes from. These different views lead to different management strategies.

However as **Operational excellence** is rooted in all of the four antagonistic disciplines, the manager's direction is often biased and does not lead to a simple and clear direction, towards operational excellence.

Let's view an example of different business cases that illustrate the different perceptions,

If a company is doing very well financially and has excellent profits year after year, but has very high employee turnover, employees who leave the company unsatisfied and frustrated and the average retention time is 1–2 years. What will the company's Chief Financial Officer conclusion be?

Is this company successful according to his judgment?

Did the management reach *Operational Excellence*?

What will the Human Resources manager or an organizational psychology expert conclude regarding the same company?

In industrial companies, real life situations are even more complex, when a previous situation is turned around by a 180° and the company barely survives financially, but the employee's contribution is outstanding and they are dedicated to the company's mission and values.

> Ask yourself what would be your observation and conclusion regarding this company's health?

What will be a financial or people's expert statement on this company?

Or another example, if there is a company that does not make any money for several years, but has fantastic promise and edge disruptive technology as opposed to a company that has high profits but stagnant technology and no innovation and entrepreneurship?

When evaluating a company's performance in light of the *Operational excellence* status, several dimensions exist. The view received from one of the four dimensions may significantly differ from the view received from another dimensions. The above perceptions reflect on management beliefs regarding the company's performance, their vision and their management decisions.

This concise guide offers a different view and concept, the view of the core business itself.

> Our operational excellence philosophy is **Unit** assessment and improvement of all four disciplines together.
>
> Improving people's contribution and motivation, financial results, industrial engineering parameters and technology as one **Unit**, a single **LEAN quality** system.

Coordinating and rating excellence as one united operation, which includes all of the components: financial, people performance innovation, output and so on, raises the company's core value.

The above scheme demonstrates the way of leading the diverse operational disciplines into one unite direction of Operational Excellence. This can be achieved through driving towards a unite vision and mission, which includes every team member in the organization.

The book's concept originated by putting together several operations content experts.

The knowledge covers over 20 years of experience in different operations disciplines and companies. There are many exciting books that come from the point of view of CEOs and General Managers, who have turned around the company's business results. Other books are from the technologist's point of view, and refer to breaking technological boundaries or revolutions in market and customers habits. There are people's behavior and organizational psychology academics and experts who analyze the role of the human element and its correlation to business breakthroughs and success. All of those books are excellent for understanding the different vectors and fields that promote or inhibit organizations from reaching *operational excellence*.

> This concise guide was written by people who practice operational excellence in their daily life.

The objective of this book is to widely share and expose practical solutions to the operations population and assist them in their daily professional dilemmas. The proposed lean, clear and harmonious solutions are achieved through advance in the financial, technological, industrial and people vectors.

The knowledge is applicable throughout all sorts of industries, from the conventional to the more advanced industries such as the Hi technology and biotechnology ones. It can serve managers, individual contributors, teams and consultants.

Operational Excellence concise guide as manual:

We describe operations building blocks in an *A to Z* order. The list contains operations core elements as production, financial elements, people management, technology processes, planning indicators and their measurement.

All the subjects are connected with same direction and objective *where* to aspire. The guide define one unite direction with the same vision and mission for *Operational Excellence* as described in Fig. 1.1.

- The book explain the reasons *why* should an operations organization aspire for excellent performance, and its consequent long term financially and operational benefits.
- For assistance in evaluating the gaps between reader's current operations status and excellent performance, few questionnaires are attached at the end of the book (Appendix C) for self-assessments and gap analysis by the different operations team.
- The guide recommends *How* to reach continuous improvement, and recommend best practices for the implementation. The recommendations are demonstrates in all the chapters as for product assurance of supply, product yield improvements, cost saving, inventory control and new technologies introduction.
- Fundamental philosophy in the concise guide are best practices as *LEAN* methodologies, *people development* and contribution, *quality* assurance, innovation in the operation and *cost* mind set. All those principals are repeated and reflected in every different subject and chapter from its specific angle and unique activity, just as aiming on the highest summit from the mountains around it.

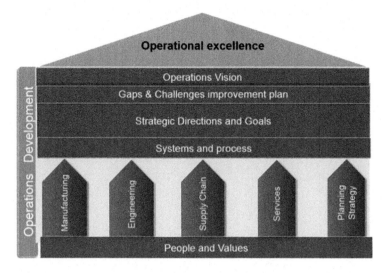

Fig. 1.1 Unite disciplines of operations and stages for implementing operational excellence

All chapters and different departments and disciplines shares the same goal which is reaching the highest summit *of operational excellence*.

As described in Fig. 1.1, the whole operations improvement structure is built on the fundamentals of the operations people culture and values. Those elements are described in details in the people and other related chapters.

Assurance of Supply (AOS)

2

2.1 Assurance of Supply Systems and Processes

The first priority and the essence of operations in the organization is *Assurance of Supply* (AOS).

AOS means providing to the customer the goods he had paid for, that he has committed to supply to his customers and has planned on, for his annual revenues. As *AOS* is the top objective and the first priority of the operations organization, it should flow in the veins of the organization. *AOS* should be embedded in the organization DNA in its culture, schedules, self-measurements and plans. It should be the top priority of every team member and the overall team goal. Operations dash boards and *break through systems* always need to reflect the actual production pace in compression to the shift's daily and weekly *AOS* output goals.

In case of non-linear production, as end of quarter or end of year peak sales, production pace should be calculated differently. We will elaborate on this specific calculation in Days of Inventory chapter. Operations weekly and monthly output goals are derived from the worldwide customers monthly supply plans, the demand and the sales plan.

> Ask yourself:
> Are quarterly and monthly sales goals are translated in to the operations weekly and daily output targets?

In cases that production are falling behind the weekly pace, special team efforts a *Task force team*, is required in order to overcome the gaps in the supply. Not meeting the required supply pace can be a result of parts and raw material shortages, or due to quality and/or technology limitations.

An important note: always we need to know how weekly output pace stands versus the weekly goals. In case of discrepancy between weekly goals and actual

© Springer International Publishing Switzerland 2016
G. Issar, L.R. Navon, *Operational Excellence*, Management for Professionals,
DOI 10.1007/978-3-319-20699-8_2

weekly output. The time till initiating a task force, will define the waste, unplanned cost and extra organization effort which requires in order to meet the weekly output goals.

> Does everyone in operations knows the weekly output pace versus the weekly goal?

2.2   Capacity and Inventory Planning for Meeting AOS

In order to minimize production and supply stops and risk for *AOS* in the future, proactive simulations reveals potential risks, limitations and bottle necks. The capacity and resources need to be analyzed according to the *Theory of Constraints* (Goldratt, 1992) in order to identify and reveal the organizational constraints and make sure that the *bottle necks* utilization and output does not fall under the weekly planned pace.

> A measure of over capacity needed to plug in to the system by design. This over capacity will serve the supply flow, in cases of increase demand or in case of halt in production.

The over capacity, also called production *burst capacity,* needs to be managed continuously according to the fluctuations in demands.

Figure 2.1 describes both situations of over and under capacity. When demand bars are under the capacity line the space between them is our over or *burst capacity*. When demand bars exceeds capacity line we face *AOS* challenge due to *under capacity* situation.

However continuous meeting of the *Assurance of Supply* goals can also be secured by proportional months of inventory. Though we need to take special caution using inventory as our solution for *Assurance of Supply* purposes. Since inventory is the company's cash, it is better if it is not held on the company production floor, or the raw materials or the finished good warehouses.

There is a rule of thumb for calculating the safe level of inventory.

> What is the lowest inventory level that you can reach, without risking **AOS**?

Every business has a different red line for weekly or monthly quantities of inventory. The right amount for weekly inventory is based on operations average recovery time after production and supply stops in the past. Production stops of all types and kinds should be included; due to quality events, technological problems, suppliers, logistics, and any other event.

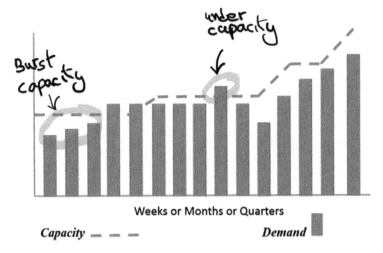

Fig. 2.1 Basic supply and demand chart

An example for safe inventory calculation:

If previous average time of a production stop was 3–4 weeks, after the resume in production, in order to get back to full production capacity after the production stop, *supply chain in* needs a week and *supply chain out* also needs a week on top of the 3–4 weeks, of the stop.

In this example, altogether we get around 5–7 weeks of relying on inventory.

Therefore, 5–7 weeks are the red line and minimum level of inventory in order to keep *Assurance of Supply* in this example most of production stop events.

> **Key Elements to Achieve Assurance of Supply:**
> Tight connection of quarterly sales plans to weekly production goals
> Full transparency and daily follow up of weekly output pace
> Daily constraint and buffer management
> Proactive task force kick off when out-put falls behind goals
> Continues reduction in number of production stops events and duration

Reference

Goldratt, E. M. (1992). *The goal: A process of ongoing improvement.* Croton-on-Hudson, NY: North River Press.

Cost of Goods (COGs)

This chapter describe how *Cost of Goods (COGs)*, can be the lighthouse and the common goal and language from the production floor technician through the engineer to the manager and up to the company CFO and General Manager.

COGs is the summation of several costs drivers in operations:

- The material cost, (Bill Of Materials)
- The labor cost,
- The Supply Chain and logistics cost
- Depreciation Cost
- The production Overhead cost

Every one of the above *COGs* component needs a separate and detailed cost reduction plan and management.

Long term *COGs* cost reduction plans results needs to reach descending value macro trend as seen in the attached Fig. 3.1 chart trend. The achieved macro trend overall reduction, trends down along years and quarters.

It is not only the overall COGs value that is reduced with time. As shown in the chart, every component by its own, BOM, Labor, and Production over head, depreciation and Supply Chain should shows decrease in their own costs year over year and quarter over quarter.

3.1   Bill of Material (BOM) Cost Reduction

In order to control the material cost in an effective and long term way, and not be frequently surprised from changes of suppliers, as price increase or quality decrease. A good foundation and Win-Win relationship with supplier needs to build. Win-Win business relationship with suppliers will discuss in details in Chap. 30. Basic common interests between the company and its strategic vendors are foundations of long term plans as *cost reduction*, *quality* and raw materials

© Springer International Publishing Switzerland 2016   11
G. Issar, L.R. Navon, *Operational Excellence*, Management for Professionals,
DOI 10.1007/978-3-319-20699-8_3

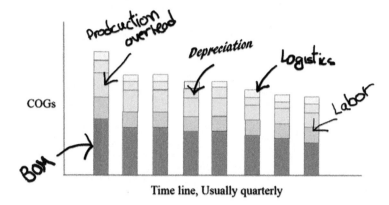

Fig. 3.1 BOM, labor, and production over head, depreciation and supply chain cost decrease

improvement. The long term cost reduction plans will bring raw material and parts price decrease in the **BOM** and will drive **COGs** decrease respectively along the years.

> Long term BOM and COGs decrease through operations projects, assures product price decrease and keeps product competitiveness in the market.

When worldwide market goods as oil or metal, or products as electronics or plastics prices are rising. Joint long term cost reduction projects of suppliers with the operations buffers and reduces world wide price increase impact on the product cost.

A breakdown of all components in **BOM** is first practical step for transparency and control of every single component price and its supplier status. Although **BOM** may contain tens of thousands of parts, prioritization and consolidations of the expensive modules will enable price control. Cost reduction plans would be effective if the thousands items list will routinely manage according to Pareto list by cost. The 20 % most expensive items in the list, which influencing the majority of cost are the first to be prioritize and work on. The top Pareto, expensive items needs technical and procurement engineering attention to substitute the expensive materials, and expensive production processes by cost effective ones. Each project needs to have its specific goal and commitment due dates for seeing the actual invoices payments decrease.

> Does the operations organization priorities cost reduction of top expensive BOM items?
> Are those items has cost reduction targets and innovative projects?

Note, we need to be aware and add to our calculations the terms of payments and raw materials inventory for actual reflection of ***BOM*** cost reduction. High inventory will postpone actual savings recognition in the financials sheets. In parallel to ***BOM*** cost reduction by *supply chain* and engineering departments, labor cost reduction efforts need to take place by the manufacturing team.

3.2   Labor Cost Reduction

Major activity of the manufacturing team should focus around *cycle time* reduction and waste elimination efforts. *Lean* and *Kaizen* improvements sessions and projects together with waste reduction in the production floor are opportunities for significant labor and material cost reductions. For cycle time reduction, the manufacturing team uses the same methodologies as supply chain and engineering applies in the ***BOM*** cost reduction. As first step manufacturing team lists every production process steps cycle time and sort them in Pareto order. Manufacturing priority and focus needs to start from top labor intensive production steps, which eventually are top opportunities for cycle time reduction. Those major opportunities needs to have cycle time reduction projects attached to them that are reviewed periodically.

Figure 3.2, chart shows an example of reducing assembly and integration cycle time from 121 days to 31 days within four consecutive quarters. Such significant decrease can achieve through structured and joint work of technician, engenders, purchasing and planning. A cycle time reduction campaign is recommended in order to motivate and generate innovative ideas. Daily follow up stand up meetings and demonstrating and reflecting improvements are important to tie in all cycle time reduction mission participants.

BOM and Cycle Time cost reduction projects are opportunity for operations people to develop innovative projects.

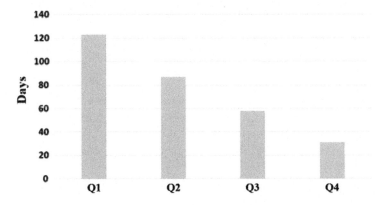

Fig. 3.2 Assembly and integration of machinery cycle time reduction

3.3   Supply Chain and Logistics Cost Reduction

We had discussed by now supply chain part in *COG*s reduction from purchasing and procurement aspects. The logistics cost reduction efforts needs segmentation in to inbound logistics, outbound logistics, and warehouse cost reduction efforts.

Every cost item in different logistics cost centers has to be check for pricing, contracts with logistics companies and formulas of the charge rates. There is major room for innovation through changing logistics routs, warehouses centralization and storage volume minimization. All these activities will significantly reduce logistics cost.

3.4   Cost Reduction of Production Overhead

Last one and most sensitive *COG*s cost reduction item in operations is production overhead cost reduction.

Here attention and carefulness is needed. While in previous discussed *COG*s cost reduction items involves negotiation with suppliers of goods and services. Also procurement, engineers and technicians applies innovation and improving flow and efficiency. With production overhead cost reduction we primarily act inside the operations organization. Production overhead exposes the operations team members, to their own effectiveness and own level of *LEAN* performances. Managers, supervisors, planners and controllers needs to check themselves for effectiveness, excess head count and redundant activities. A self-judgment is more complicate to apply than negotiating with vendor on parts cost reduction, or innovate cost reduction activity.

As reducing production overhead is important and sensitive subject, it needs special attention, professional and long term thinking. Before starting production overhead improvements we need keep in mind that operations team motivation and will to win spirit, is critical building block for *operational excellence*. Not internalizing this value while dealing with people jobs will offend atmosphere of trust. Improving operations effectiveness and reducing redundancy needs to be inflight of the following understandings:

- Need to involve team recommendations for organization adjustments in order to learn on variety of opportunities and keep team engagement with the expected changes.
- Over proportion of production overhead, turns to a burden on the product **COG**s, it also slows down operations effectiveness with none added value activities. (See Chaps. 20 and 21)
- Lean and *Kaizen* sessions significantly helps to re- define and consolidate activities in operation.
- Improving production overhead creates job rotations, new career development opportunities and overall organizational freshness and growth.

3.4.1   Start: Stop–Continue

An applicable methodology for refresh and re defining operational structures when production overhead cost reduction is needed, is Start, Stop, and Continue session. A joint team thinking defines what activities are critical to continue with. What activities are no longer relevant and can be stopped. And what activities are missing and needs to be started with.

Decision Support Systems (DSS)

4

In order to reach *Operational Excellence*, we need to continuously improve the critical knobs of operations performance, such as *AOS*, *COG*s, People's contribution and *yields* and *inventory* levels. Results are improved through continuous monitoring of critical activities results and reflecting them to the operations team, as well as by setting new targets. The mechanism for defining and measuring operations performance is through measuring a few, correct, operations *Key Performance Indicators* (*KPI*).

> Routine **KPI**s review secure operations reaching and exceeding planned goals on a daily, weekly, monthly and quarterly basis.

> The tools which measure, calculate and reflect operations **KPI** results are the **Decision Support Systems**. From daily micro resolution to annual macro trends.

Continuous attention and following up on operations *DSS* is as important as looking at our car speedometer, GPS or watch in order to plan our arrival time at a destination. *DSS* are our speedometer, watch and navigation systems. The differences between effective *DSS* and redundant measuring systems and reports are in the following three elements:

1. Importance
2. Accuracy
3. Usage

© Springer International Publishing Switzerland 2016
G. Issar, L.R. Navon, *Operational Excellence*, Management for Professionals,
DOI 10.1007/978-3-319-20699-8_4

Ask yourself; how many of the Decision Support reports existing in operations are critical and used daily?

4.1   Importance

An organization can have numerous *KPI* presented in various reports, on screen charts and in the web. They are not necessarily the right decision support factors and critical reports, sometimes those *KPI* and reports are not viewed, by the operations team member, as routinely as they should be in order to influence their daily decisions. We can consider the *DSS* important if it measures and reflects the following:

Critical performance parameters, throughout a period of time, in which we can improve their results.

For example, if the *DSS* does not alert a crisis in a system for several years—this system is not an <u>important</u> system. Another example can be a parameter that was defined as critical during the development phase and remains above target constantly, for years. Continuously measuring a parameter that does not change, or not alerting before a crisis means that the parameter is not a critical one.

4.2   Accuracy

If the *DSS* reveals a crisis after it happens—the specific system is not *accurate* or, it is accurate but was neglected. An example of inaccurate measuring is, maintenance time based equipment versus the workload base. Equipment maintenance routines are usually time based, preventive maintenance activities are conducted routinely, on a weekly, monthly or quarterly basis. In a situation when the same equipment runs two processes and one of the processes is more intensive for the equipment, time based equipment maintenance will miss treatments of equipment that runs the intensive process, and we will choose *inaccurate* parameters for our *DSS* measurements. Another example is, *DSS* for measuring production time. If production time measurement is based on a daily *cycle time,* a linear based percentage *DSS* will show at the middle of the time period that we have completed 50 % of the product, this will not be *accurate* if the production line is not linear and if the time required to perform half of the tasks is more than half of the production time. In such a non-linear production line, over or under than 50 % of the product production should be completed after 50 % of the total time.

4.3   DSS Usage

The third important *DSS* criteria is, *DSS* usage. An important rule before improving or implementing a new *DSS* is, to check the report usage. Teams may create many reports and IT systems, if the *DSS* reveals a crisis late, after it happens, it means that the system was not periodically reviewed by the operations team and during the operations meetings. In this case, the *DSS* may have measured the *important* and accurate parameters but, it was not routinely used. Such event can also happen with 'product end life' reports, equipment and process alerts, risk assessments and lessons learned. In these cases, when *DSS* and reports are important but not critical, we need to apply routines to sustain and review the report before an operations crises occurs, due to neglect.

> In simple words:
> Effective Decision Support Systems prevents un-predicted events as: production stops, cost increase quality events and overall task forces in the operations.

4.4   Major DSS and KPIs at the Different Operations Departments

Every department in the operation has to have its own *KPI* embedded in the *DSS*. A KPI parameters nominator should measure the actual performance value in regard to the *operational excellence* stretched goal or to references which appear in the denominator of the report.

The supply chain team needs to proactively monitor, through their *DSS*, raw material quality, arrival versus plans and availability, supplier's stability and *BOM* cost, logistics and warehousing quality and costs.

Production should measure the *cycle time* by using the production floor systems, it should also measure product tree BOM system material and parts quality, material replenishment rates, cost changes, parts quality and material non-standard activities. Decision support systems should monitor the production's process accuracy and the deviations from process control baselines, and alert accordingly. Engineering needs to reflect the product's stabilization, *cost* and *quality* improvements, *NPI* readiness and configuration status in regard to the product tree.

Services need to reflect customer's satisfaction, product stability and the ownership product cost.

In their *DSS,* Planning need to show *Inventory*, supply and demand statuses as well as financial trends, such as *Gross Margin*, *MOH*, department spending, capital expenditure, scrap and more.

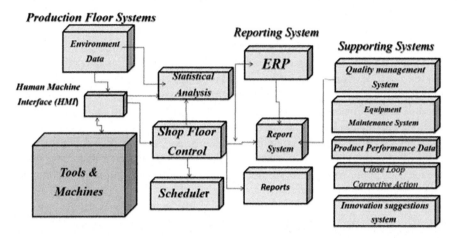

Fig. 4.1 Decision support system including production plant, support systems and reports

Figure 4.1 represents the structure of the database and information systems behind the decision support systems. On the left side of the scheme are the production line, tool and machine, information systems. In the center are the statistical analysis, scheduling and ERP systems. The right part of the scheme describes all of the supporting systems, such as quality and product performance data storage.

All the data and system, from product raw material through the production phase and till performance at the customer's site, are routed into the analyzing and report generating systems. This scheme represents how critical it is to manage a diverse operations system, with an enormous database, in a structured, accurate and precise way.

Not collecting and measuring the data of critical and precise information paths, can cause losses in the operations goals like AOS, Cost, Quality, People motivation and Cycle Time Reduction.

Defining and crystalizing the critical KPIs in a few Decision Support Systems, continuously improves continuously operations performance.

Drum, Buffer, Rope and Days of Inventory (DOI) Control

5

This simple combination, of planning **Days of Inventory (DOI)**[1] according to the **Theory of constraint (TOC)** (Goldratt, 1992) rules, is an effective formula and a practical planning tool. Since the logic behind the **TOC** is to optimize the production line's inventory, applying this logic to the practical operational calculations and daily practices assures a minimal amount of inventory days. In order to implement the theory of constraint (Goldratt, 1992) in production planning, it is recommended to practice the *Drum, Buffer and Rope* constraint management methodology.

5.1 What Is the Drum, Buffer, Rope, Methodology?

The *Drum Beat* of a production line is defined as the shift, the daily or weekly output pace, which adds up to the monthly output and supply goals. The *Drum beat* can be measured as the amount of product units, as 20 machines per week or as the number of tons or devices per week, gallons, drums or grams of chemical. The line's *Drum Beat* number is dictated by the line's constraint. We need to calculate and design the production line in a way that the line's constraint can always supply the product's planned demand. The constraint always needs to be managed and kept in its highest utilization, in order to always be able to provide the *Drum Beat* quantity.

For example: Fig. 5.1 describes a part of a production line which consists of three production steps. The *constraint* of those three steps is the middle step's capacity, which limits the line output to 650 units per week. This line constraint

---

[1] DOI Calculation

Quarterly DOI = Inventory/Cost of Goods Sold * 90 (days)

For calculation the annual DOI, 90 days can be replaced by 360 days and the COGs needs to be the total yearly COGs.

© Springer International Publishing Switzerland 2016
G. Issar, L.R. Navon, *Operational Excellence*, Management for Professionals,
DOI 10.1007/978-3-319-20699-8_5

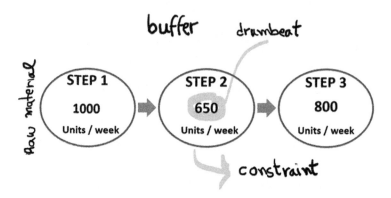

Fig. 5.1 Production process example, with its constraints and consequent *Drum Beat*

dictates the line's *Drum Beat* as a maximum of 650 units per week, and we need to ensure that STEP 2 does not produces less.

In order to ensure that the line output is always 650 units per week, we need to feed the constraint continuously without stopping. The **Work in process (WIP)** which is kept before the constraint, will ensure that the constraint always works in its maximum capacity. If a line stop happens, in an upstream step before the constraint, a few days or shifts of work will amount up before the constraint keeps the constraint fed, and until the line resumes working. The amount of work before the constraint is called the *Buffer*. The *Buffer* will ensure continuous production of the constraint in spite of upstream line stops. The third element in the *Drum, Buffer,* and *Rope* methodology connects the constraint to the weekly amount of incoming raw materials from the beginning of production. The theoretical connection between the line's start of production to the constraint, ties and tunes the constraint's capacity with the incoming amount of raw materials. Through this connection, line entrance allows neither more nor less material than the *drum beat* out-put. Tying a connection between the constraint and the beginning of the line, with same production *drum beat* amount, is called the *"rope"*. The *rope* verifies that the production line's first steps are exactly subordinate to the fluctuations in the constraint's output performance (Fig. 5.2).

In production terms: with the rope system, the constraint will not be "flooded" because excess material enters the production line and it will not be "starved" because not enough material enters the production line. If we want to connect the *AOS* and the *inventory* and *constraint* management logics and phrase it in one sentence, we can say that:

Flooding the *constraint* with excess material will cause *excess inventory* in the line, while starving the constraint will cause an *AOS* miss.

There are a few practices that we need to check in when operating a production line according to the Theory of Constraint (Goldratt, 1992):

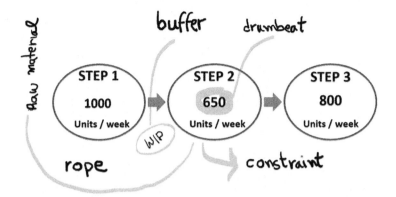

Fig. 5.2 Tying incoming material with a "*rope*" to the constraint

- Does everyone in the operation know which steps in the production line are the *line constraints*?
- What is the production line *Drum Beat*?
- Does the planning department keep a *buffer* before the *constraint*?
- Is the quantity of material that enters the line connected to the constraint?

5.2   Drum, Buffer, Rope and Sales Volume

An interesting situation occurs when the product's sales and market are the production's constraint. In this situation, production capacity can exceed the market's demand. In such a case the *rope* needs to be tied between the sales plan and incoming materials to the production floor. New batches of raw material or parts will only enter the production line's first station, after the finished goods leave the warehouse, or go out the end of the line, to the customer. In this way we will keep the situation as described in the chart marked Fig. 5.3—production line is balanced and ensures inventory is in control.

In Fig. 5.3, we can review a real production line's situation and results, during 3 years, where inventory was reduced from a 120 days to 60 days. In this case, like the one described, market size and sales were the line's constraint. By applying the philosophy of the Theory of Constraint (Goldratt, 1992) and the *Drum, Buffer, Rope* principals, the *rope* connected the sales *Drum Beat* to the incoming pace of raw material to the line.

Applying the *TOC* principles, in this case, enabled cutting the inventory days by half within 1 year, and keeping it at around 65 days.

Planning the monthly production by calculating the Drum, Buffer and Rope, ensures the existence of a minimal Inventory and optimizes constraint feed.

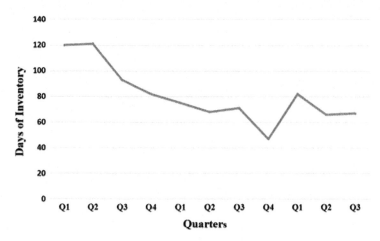

Fig. 5.3 Inventory reduction and control by using *Drum Buffer* and *Rope* Theory of Constraint principles

Reference

Goldratt, E. M. (1992). *The goal: A process of ongoing improvement.* Croton-on-Hudson, NY: North River Press.

emails (The *LEAN* Version)   6

6.1   The Importance in Manage and Not to be Managed by emails

Due to the times, nowadays not many of the operations team members have experienced the world of operations with any means of communication other than emails. As they were not there before emails became the organization's ultimate tool for communication. This may be the reason, why people hesitate to use practices that can reduce email disturbances and restrict their governess over the daily schedule.

These practices, can assist operation team members who are more influenced by emails, and can improve their control over their time management and over the portion of time they dedicate to work on their emails.

There are many practical and technical tips for reducing the influence of hundreds of incoming emails on our priorities, daily schedule and planned output. In this chapter, we will focus more on the principles and less on the tactics that can help, the operations manager or team member, focus on the most important emails.

Many people feel paralyzed by the numerous emails they receive along the day. At the end of the work day, they realize that they have not achieved or advanced, their core or important, objectives as they had planned to. A combination of the '*seven habits*' practice and of the '*theory of constraint* (Goldratt, 1992)' is the *LEAN* answer to efficient and effective email management in an operations daily routine. Working proactively on the important emails will always decrease and prevent *AOS* crises, quality failures events and *COG* decline, several weeks before they take place.

© Springer International Publishing Switzerland 2016   25
G. Issar, L.R. Navon, *Operational Excellence*, Management for Professionals,
DOI 10.1007/978-3-319-20699-8_6

Fig. 6.1 Subject sorting by
their level of importance and
urgency (from Covey, 1996)

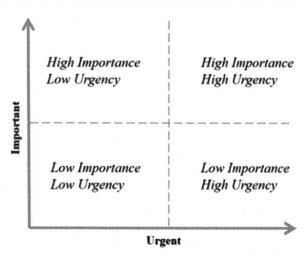

6.2   Sorting emails by Their Importance

When we prioritize our emails according to their importance, we can first focus our attention on the subjects with the highest importance levels and highest levels of urgency. There are four 'importance and urgency' combination quadrants: Important and urgent, Urgent but unimportant, Important but not urgent and subjects or emails that are neither urgent nor important (Covey, 1996) (Fig. 6.1).

> email should be sorted according to their position in the importance/urgent quadrants.

The first emails that need to get our attention, are those in quadrant one and quadrant two, important and urgent and urgent but unimportant. We should try not to deal with emails according to the 'first in, first read priority'. The urgent but unimportant emails need to be cleared out of the way as soon as possible, in order to free the way for dealing with the important materials.

6.3   Identifying the emails that Deal with Operational Constraints

We need to identify the operation's constraints, and immediately read the emails related to them.

Constraints arise in operations on a daily basis, on a certain day it may be an *AOS* problem due to material availability, on another occasion it may be the technology task force or critical parameters that have deviated from the process control limits. A potential decrease in the **Gross Margin** due to cost increase or an urgent customer complaint may be major subjects of importance. All of these matters are in emails that fall into the important and urgent category. After we deal with the important and urgent emails, we need to pay attention to same important subjects which are currently less urgent. Usually those emails will look, at first glance, as minor concerns of small issues, they may concern certain deviations in the performance of a process or a production parameter or any other important but not urgent subject. The tricky thing about those emails is, that we can never know whether and when they will turn out to be the next crisis.

> Working systematically on the important but not urgent emails, will proactively prevent the next crises in the operations from happening.

Preventing the creation of the next task force, by building healthy and high quality operation fundamentals, starts with putting focus on the important subjects in our incoming mail box. Sometimes people misconnect *operational excellence* with intensive email correspondence and transactions, and many emails, which contain detailed updates on the task forces activities, are considered by mistake as a high performance level of operation in the organization. Actually, *operational excellence* is achieved by the exact opposite of numerous, urgent emails and simultaneously managing of several crises events. A smoothly flowing operational activity is characterized by preventative emails and not by reactive emails, and represents the organization's strength and robustness.

Many task forces, crises and emails characterize an unstable operational infrastructure, which easily and frequently falls into a crisis mode. An excess of high priority emails draws people's attention away from their quality and preventive work and prevents it from getting done.

> Lean communication and fewer taskforces, represent a strong and preventive infrastructure, which are the principals of operational excellence.

By continuously eliminating the root causes to the operation's crises, the amount of task forces is reduced, over time. Consequently, crisis communications and emails are reduced and become minimal. The 'proactive quality events preventative methodology' will be discussed in depth in Chap. 27.

The rest of the emails, other than the proactive important subjects which require urgent attention and actions, can be reviewed in a less frequent manner. For the unimportant and not urgent emails the recommendation is to use the delete option on the keyboard with no hesitation. If the subject of the email is not important it draws our attention away from the important subjects. The **Lean** way for achieving success in an operation is to focus and concentrate on the operation's key vectors, such as **AOS**, *quality, gross margin* and *people's motivation and contribution.*

Waste mails which circle in the organization occupy the team's time with activities which have no added value, and draw people's concentration away from the important email subjects towards non -value communications. We all prefer maximum concentration on operational subjects, which is why *emails* need to reflect the seriousness, focus and professionalism in operations.

References

Covey, S. (1996). *The seven habits of highly effective people.* Tel Aviv: Oram.
Goldratt, E. M. (1992). *The goal: A process of ongoing improvement.* Croton-on-Hudson, NY: North River Press.

Empowerment

7

> An environment that encourages employee empowerment will promote the employee as well as the whole team to excellent achievements.

Managers are key figures who affect the behaviors and conduct of employees in the work place. This is why managers has an important role in creating the appropriate environment for their employees and influences their development. Empowerment is the only way that employees can maximize their own potential.

The key to empowerment is: creating mutual, autonomous, trusting and authentic relationships.

Building these principles for empowerment is relevant to any relationship a manager establishes with the different factors around him.

7.1 Why Should a Manager, Invest in Empowerment?

- Empowerment enables an increase of the employee's responsibilities and expands his areas of influence.
- Empowerment increases employee's sense of responsibility, ambitiousness and motivation.
- Empowerment encourages employee's creativity, innovation and initiative
- Empowerment promotes operational excellence.

But if we expand the contribution that empowerment has on the employee themselves, we can see that the empowering manager has the same benefits as the one's listed above.

© Springer International Publishing Switzerland 2016
G. Issar, L.R. Navon, *Operational Excellence*, Management for Professionals,
DOI 10.1007/978-3-319-20699-8_7

7.2   What Empowered Employees Allow Their Managers to Do?

When employees are empowered they allow their managers to:

- Expand the responsibilities and circles of administrative effect. If beforehand the managers focused on thinking and tactical planning, having empowered workers frees them of that, and allows them to inspect the processes and influences in a more systemic manner and to free time for strategic thinking.
- Empowered employees allow their managers to develop more administrative, organizational and systemic directions.
- Having teams, in general, and employees as individuals empowered creates high team capacities, which allows the manager to develop opportunities for innovative thinking and initiative that would not have developed if the team did not have the developed skills.

7.3   Characteristics of Empowering Managers

An analysis of a wide range of interviews with managers who are considered empowering, and conversations with workers about what they regard to be an empowering manager allowed us to identify several characteristics of empowering managers:

1. Empowering managers recruit workers who they can learn from—in most cases our natural tendency as managers is to recruit people that are similar to us. They are the ones who we claim to "chemistry" with.
   There are even executives who for fear of recruiting a worker who has a certain advantage over them, will consider their own well-being before that of the organization and will not recruit such a worker despite of his added value.
   Empowering managers are those who during the recruiting process look for workers who one can learn from. The managerial understanding is that these sort of employees can bring added value, not only to the task/project/role they were hired for, an employee that one can learn from expands the whole team's circle of capabilities and through that can enable leveraging of team performance.
2. Empowering managers run continuous employee development processes (on the personal, team and organizational levels)
   Empowering managers are executives who look and lead the process of personal development among their employees and teams throughout the whole year and not only at the point of time defined by the organization.
   The meaning of this is that their attitude towards personal growth is that it is an ongoing process where difficulties can arise as well as success.
   Therefore they will invest time in active coaching of their employees in order to allow them to acquire and utilize their potential.

They will do so in several methods, such as: providing learning guidelines, allocating resources to training as well as to development of skills and qualifications, allowing employee involvement in the decision making process in order to make them partners etc.

3. When executives give *End to End Ownership*- give responsibly and authority to their employees they actually increase the employee's level of commitment and responsibly for action.

   Granting the authority sends the employee a message that he has the abilities, skills and knowledge to lead himself to success, and the company to achievements.

   Empowered employees know they are responsible for their decisions and for the results of their work. People who are determined and responsible have the freedom to decide how to do their work and to initiate further processes.

   They have the power to make decisions that are relevant to their work.

   There for these employees will constantly look for ways to develop and implement constant improvement processes from the point of view of operational excellence.

4. Empowering managers are tolerant to employee's mistakes and willing to take chances—An empowering manager enhances his employee's ability to choose, and makes decisions that affect their work, and subsequently initiate processes. Therefore an empowering manager creates a work environment that is not intimidated by criticism, a prerequisite to encouraging creativity, innovation and initiative.

   In such an environment the manager gives the employees the chance to be themselves and to experience, which allows them the opportunity to learn through experiences, learn from mistakes and continuous learning.

5. Empowering managers support the ongoing learning of their employees—in order to promote processes of learning from mistakes, as mentioned above, empowering managers allocate a fair amount of their time to learning guidance for their employees, because they know that an investment in the short term will bring many advantages in the medium and long term.

   But, creating a learning platform in the wide sphere of work in an organization is manifested in a range of formal and informal learning processes. In order to empower an employee's skills, learning is a valuable and meaningful channel in building the professional confidence and self-perception of the organization's employee.

   Therefore, during the ongoing dialogue the empowering executives have with their employees, the executives make sure they identify the fields in which it is necessary to impart knowledge, skills and abilities and accordingly allocate resources and operate all networking channels: formal and informal learning channels in the organization to support this learning (such as: acquiring an education, mentoring).

6. Empowering managers provide ongoing feedback (positive and for improvement)—the feedback is one of the most meaningful tools in the process of empowering an employee. Empowering executives provide ongoing feedback

to their employees, not only within the framework of the structured annual process of performance evaluation, if such a process exists.

Providing feedback is part of their ongoing work routine and can be expressed both in a positive feedback and an improvement feedback.

Feedback—Information provided to the individual regarding the degree to which his/her actions and behaviors are effective in promoting expected outcomes or results. It is a basic, crucial managerial tool for promoting employee motivation and engagement:

- *Positive Feedback*—Information provided in order to strengthen desired behaviors and encourage their repetition by conveying approval.
- *Feedback for Improvement*—Information provided in order to prevent undesirable behavior. Usually includes an explanation regarding a behavior's in effectiveness in promoting desirable outcomes.

7. Empowering managers create an organizational climate that supports establishment of conditions that promote empowerment- this sort of organizational climate develops when there is a solid foundation of trust between the manager and his employees.

   The meaning of this is that, the empowering manager is required to have high abilities and skills as an empathetic listener; receiving and providing feedback; sharing information and involving the employees in the decision making process; transparency, evaluation of every employee's contribution and openness.

It is important to emphasize that, empowerment starts first of all in the executive mindset. Therefore, executives who want to develop empowerment skills and empowering executives who wish to strengthen their empowering skills, should ask themselves the following questions-

- What does empowerment mean to me? As a manager? On the employee level? On the team level?
- What are the empowering skills that as manager I need to develop in order to promote the empowerment of my employees?
- How do I translate/convert empowerment into practice? How does my management conception of myself as an empowering manager be reflected in the "field"

Enterprise Resource Planning (ERP)

8

A new class of packaged application software has been introduced to operations during the last decade. It consolidates all of the company's business operations activities under a single system, usually called 'enterprise resource planning system' (ERP).

8.1 ERP Content and Evolvement

These comprehensive, packaged software solutions seek and integrate a complete range of the business's processes and functions in order to present a full and central view of the business as a united, single system.

An ERP system is defined as a fully integrated business management system which covers functional areas of the enterprise such as, Logistics, Production, Finance, Accounting and Human Resources.

Some of the solutions also embed customer relations management and their functionalities, in them.

ERP organizes and integrates operations processes and information flow, in order to make optimum use of resources, such as people, materials, money and production machines.

ERP evolved from a system known as MRP II (Manufacturing Requirement Planning) with integration of information from vendor, customer and manufacturer. MRP is a technique that connects several major operational systems and processes. MRP exposes the end product demands obtained from the Master Production Schedule (MPS) in order to receive given product specifications and content.

In order to receive product components, a product tree is derived from the Bill of Materials (BOM), also stored in the MRP. The BOM transforms it into a schedule for the ordering and arrival of materials and parts. Ordering also includes calculating and considering inventory levels, through pulling and replenishing the produced material. The ERP system does not manage transactions separately, as a stand-alone activity, but considers them to be interlinked processes that build a whole business.

© Springer International Publishing Switzerland 2016

33

G. Issar, L.R. Navon, *Operational Excellence*, Management for Professionals,
DOI 10.1007/978-3-319-20699-8_8

Other important enabling technologies for ERP systems are Workflow, Work Group, Electronic Data Interchange (EDI), Data warehousing etc.

8.2   ERP Functions, Features and Advantages

Major features of ERP and their benefits are:

- ERP provides versatility and enables parallel work on several platforms, facilities, manufacturing modes, currencies and also several lingual facilities.
- ERP supports strategic and business planning activities. It supports the operational planning as well as following up on execution of activities, such as production, finished goods shipment and their results.
- From the finance point of view, ERP integrates all financial information into a single version for all the systems and users in the different departments and levels of the organization.
- ERP integrates the customer order flow and the information along the flow. From the early stage of an order being entered through sales, until finance send an invoice and receive the payments. Orders can be tracked easily by operations who deliver the goods, from procurement throughout manufacturing and shipment to the customer.
- Of course ERP is essential for inventory management, as any small or large quantity of material and parts ordered, supplied to production or scrapped is reduced and replenished from the inventory. Real time order fulfillment and transparency is the only way to control and reduce inventory.
- ERP is a major component of the company and of the operation Decision Support System, it provides a real-time, enterprise-wide view of the business, for faster and more effective decision making.
- Since ERP enables constant financial transparency of product cost, every purchase of a BOM item causes flags on price increase or decrease, cost control and reduction of operating and administrative costs is very efficient.
- ERP parts and material supply methodologies, such as Just in Time, can be implemented and can consequently shorten production lead times and delivery times.
- ERP consolidates multiple permissions and security procedures into a single framework, which reduces the risk of losing or exposing sensitive data.

8.3   Caution Needed in ERP Implementation

Implementation of the ERP system is a very complex project, which involves every team and activity across the organization, therefore the project needs to involve structural changes in management's thinking and actions. The organization needs to clearly list the key business advantages which it expects to be supported by the system. The rest the organization should follow the software process and if possible the 'best practices' within its sector. Keeping existing processes, that people are used to, and customizing the software accordingly reduces the short term learning time and rejection, but it increases costs in the long term. ERP implementation in industries, also in world leading companies, has involved several cases which ended in high costs and some operative failures. In these cases, since the project took longer than planned, companies lost sales during the year of the implementation.

8.4   Examples for Proven Practices for ERP Implementation and Assimilation

There are ways to minimize the risks of failure with ERP projects, and to reduce objections from the users.

8.4.1   ERP Project Complexity

The first important point to consider is the difference between the ERP Project and any other project.

In an ERP project, we put company operations as our first priority, as all sub systems must operate harmoniously. The users need to understand, that in ERP many people in the company will use most of the information entered in to the system by a single user.

For **Example**: The warehouse keeper enters the quantity of a materials received, purchasing will use this data to approve vendor invoices, production control will use it to issue a pick list and planning and finance will use it to calculate inventory and gross margin. The first stage in an ERP Project is making the decision to start searching for a system to replace the existing system or programs. The company's management commitment should be received in an early stage of the project. Management commitment is critical for the success of the project, it will be tested during the execution phase and especially when transforming from the previous system to the new one. We need to try to be as realistic as possible regarding time and money investments required throughout the project. Also we need to be careful, at the RFP (Request for Proposal) stage, people might try to simplify and give expensive and unrealistic timeline goal estimations.

8.4.2   Request for Proposal

RFP is one of the most important stages, in this stage we define the company's needs and get our user groups and key users involved for the first time. Many processes in the company are generic and should not be focused upon (Purchasing, Warehouse management, Finance etc.) but, they need to be written, as they will be replaced with similar ERP processes. Also, we need to identify the specific processes which give our company its business advantage. Each user group should read and give input to each part of the process within their function or department, that way we gain their involvement and commitment (Soft change management) and also a tool to later evaluate the software checked. With every software that has reached the final stage of RFP we should conduct a *CRP (Conference room pilot)*. During the pilot, each user group should participate in their part of the process, and grade each process. This way we receive the involvement of the users, their commitment and their first exposure to the software again.

8.4.3   Pilot and Testing of the System

Another recommendation for piloting and testing of the system, is using the built in *'Best Practice'* process in the ERP system. Customizing and making modifications, which are not defined as competitive, due to requests of users during the process, will increase the cost of the software, the length of the project and may have bugs.

We need to be aware that customizing and responding to users requests, reduces their resistance to the project. Doing the 'best practice' will be the ultimate test to whether we have the management's commitment.

The second pilot which must performed before going live, should be on a test environment with real company data. During this pilot, we should be able to perform all main processes, from procurement to payment and offers to receive. This process should be repeated until full success, since it is the only proof we have that the company will perform properly when going live. There are usually two general requests in such a project 1. To perform the project in stages 2. To leave the old system running.

Implementing ERP in one phase has many advantages. Since, during the ERP implementation project most of the company employees are doing their daily work on top of their duties in the project, time is limited. As for keeping the old system, it is usually only necessary to leave the old system running in view mode for few users. During the first stage, before the system is completely free of issues and people are accustomed to it, there is usually some dissatisfaction, at this stage the project timeline and costs need to be considered carefully and not be exceeded by supporting minor troubleshooting.

One last piece of advice is to use ERP as part of the organization's *BPR (Business process reengineering)*. During the system's entire life, there will always be more processes and modules the organization can implement which were not on the project's initial critical path. This and re implementing existing processes, bring improvements and added value to the organization.

Failure Mode and Effect Analysis (FMEA) 9

There is permanent debate in business operations on quality failures, scrap and losses predictability and prevention. Many times people ask, how can we prevent future and non-quality events to occur?

People in operations are frustrated from the unexpected appearance of quality events, of scrap and task- forces, and looking for proactive prevention tools to significantly reduce them.

A practical FMEA approach is that although deviations in quality have statistical variability, those quality and process deviations, have common dependencies and statistical commonalities that can be predicted and prevented.

Some of the commonalities are equipment performance and personnel knowledgeability and proficiency. We will elaborate on control of the statistical nature and variability of performance in operations in the section on control of *variability*.

In *FMEA* methodology we proactively assess potential failures. An Organization that wishes to improve its quality performances uses FMEA methodology frequently. Reduction of quality failures happens after quality events occur and through implementing lessons learned recommendations and using conclusions for FMEA analysis. By using *FMEA* methodology we do not wait for a lesson and learn post the event, in order to prevent the next repeated failure. *FMEA* is based on assumption that in every product, and in its production process we have potential failure build in due to its variability and to the statistical nature of operations.

It is wiser to learn potential failures in advance and try to prevent them from happening. In order to segregate between potential failures, we need to sort them by their potential effect. While using *FMEA* methodology we start estimating potential failures from factors with the highest potential effect to the ones with the lowest potential effect.

Is FMEA a routine practice among engineers and technicians in the operations to prevent reveal and prevent potential failures?

© Springer International Publishing Switzerland 2016
G. Issar, L.R. Navon, *Operational Excellence*, Management for Professionals,
DOI 10.1007/978-3-319-20699-8_9

For analyzing potential failures engineering has to know in depth the product, process and production machines potential risks. After we had mapped all potential failures we rank them according to the highest potential. For the highest potential failure we need to develop a risk reduction plan and implement the plan.

In order to sort the failure risk by their potential effect we use a measurement called RPN.

We define the potential failure *Risk Priority Number (RPN)*, according the potential severity, potential occurrence and the detectability of the potential failure. All those three numbers are multiply one by the other. After we had defined the RPN value, we build and develop RPN reduction plan. Then we can follow up on the decrease in potential failure as the preventive actions takes place until RPN number decreases.

9.1   Examples for Using FMEA

Product engineering will use the FMEA in order to prevent product malfunction, safety hazardous of the product or reduction in product life span.

Process engineers will reveal and reduce through FMEA potential process deviations quality events and production stops due to process and quality deviations. Also potential process non-quality events that will harm the product performance, life span and reliability.

Equipment and tool engineers will use the FMEA in order to review all production module of the production tools and the risk for causing process deviations and harming the product, due to the tool malfunction.

We should perform *FMEA* process of brain storming on the potential failure effect and rating them in a teams and involve several technical members with special dedicated time.

9.2   Major Steps of the *FMEA*

- Team brain storm of the potential mode
- List of the potential effects
- Rank the potential effect by severity of the effect
- Rank by the occurrence of the effect
- Rank by detection
- Calculation of the RPN
- Development of the action plan
- Work on the action and review the reduction in the RPN

After taking FMEA actions, number of potential failure and RPNs reduces, the product, process and machines are more stable and operations less vulnerable to unpredicted cost.

9.3 Full FMEA Process Steps

Fig. 9.1.

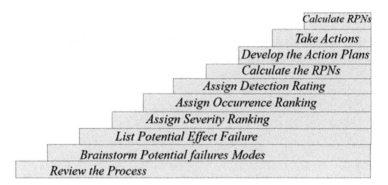

Fig. 9.1 Full FMEA process steps

Gross Margin (GM)

10

10.1 Gross Margin and the Company's Financial Health

Among the numerous number which appear in the financial business reviews, reports and analyses, there is one financial number that managers in operations can identify with and stick to, as their ultimate financial indicator.

Gross Margin (GM) is the financial indicator that ties operations to the company's business reality. We calculate GM by deducting from the product prices and sales quantities, which creates the P&L revenue top line, the operation's direct and indirect spending costs. Knowing the positive gross margin values and managing them, assists operations in navigating through economic changes and in reaching positive financial results. Operations team members are exposed, but have less influence than other financial lines in the company's P&L, such as the revenue top line, sales, administration or R&D costs. Operations financial goal is to meet assurance of supply with the lowest COG and MOH possible, in order to reach the highest Gross Margin and support high and profitable P&L results.

> By keeping Assurance of Supply, and high Gross Margins, the product's financial competitiveness and strength will flow through to the bottom profit line.

While companies, operating profit and bottom line, are subjected to other company activities, such as R&D, management, marketing and sales costs, the *GM* is mostly influenced by the operations activities. The best and most effective way to improve the operations financial performances and excel in them, is by making the *GM* goals, in percentage, a transparent and hands on tool for the organization's operations. By doing so the gross margin goal numbers become a tool for the operations manager, well as for every working group. A tool which can measure all of their expenses and activities according to the cost reduction goals.

© Springer International Publishing Switzerland 2016
G. Issar, L.R. Navon, *Operational Excellence*, Management for Professionals,
DOI 10.1007/978-3-319-20699-8_10

Ask yourself whether everyone in the operations team knows the quarterly gross margin improvement goals?

Note: If there is a risk of leakage of sensitive business information, gross margin improvement goals can be published in relative percentages. The goals communicated to the operations team, can be the delta of improvement in *GM* percentages. For example, Instead of communicating a goal of reaching a *GM* of 50 %, we can communicate an objective of a 5.5 % *GM* improvement goal. In this way, though teams have a specific numeric goal, the company P&L results are not exposed.

10.2   Setting Gross Margin Improvement Goals

Setting ambitious gross margin goals starts with benchmarking with the industry's competition, and setting significant goals for improvement. In this way, the operations team's aim is high, to be a leading operational organization with a high *GM,* in reference to its industry's benchmark. The *GM* improvement goal should be an overall *KPI* for the improvement of the whole operation, as well as a proportional goal for every one of its departments. Financial numbers need to be translated into operation indicators, which can be measured daily. An important point, that we are sometimes less aware of, is that the production floor people and the engineering measured KPI use a different vocabulary than the one used is in P&L discussions. Just like yield and cycle time numbers cannot be add directly to the P&L numbers, and they need to converted into GM percentages, while setting gross margin percentage improvement goals, to every department regarding its known operational KPI, the same conversion language needs to be applied.

Manufacturing needs to convert their portion, of the gross margin improvements points, to specific *Cycle Time* improvement goals in days. Engineers need to translate the correlation between every yield point improvement or decrease, to its correct amount of money in the product's *COG* and Gross Margin percentages. Annual yield improvements goals and scrap reduction goals need to be calculated according to the gross margin improvement points required.

The *Supply Chain* needs to continuously measure the costs, reduction gains, of the *Bill of Material* for gross margin points improvement. The same calculations need to be made in MOH cost improvements and department's expense reductions.

Does every department has its points of gross margin improvement translated in to their measured **KPI**s as **cycle Time**, material scrap and BOM cost reduction?

10.3   Gross Margin Improvements Through Innovation

Improving *GM* points and setting ambitious goals, are a major opportunity to promote the operations teams *innovation*. Cost reduction initiatives, such as eliminating non added value operational steps and applying LEAN processes will save money and reduces costs. Making improvements, by increasing the yield results and by reducing the amount of scrapped material, are always opportunities for professionals, and innovative engineers and teams to excel in the implementation of breakthrough solutions.

> Continuous improvement of the **GM** through numerous routine incremental improvement projects is also called **Kaizen**.

Once routine *GM* improvement systems are in place, and every individual in the organization has a cost improvement and a cost reduction goal, in his specific working area, and all of the personal and departmental goals funnel and sum up to quarterly improvements in the amount of *GM* savings, than, the operations will lead a positive improvement in the company's overall P&L by generating a larger positive *flow through* to the bottom line.

> The operations **GM** amount, is broken down in to team saving and improvement goals, and then flows back and is summed up to reach the increase of earnings in the profit line.

Hiring Practices for Operations

11

In recent years it is widely accepted that people are the most critical and valuable element of every organization. Hiring the right people, retaining them in the operations, while enhance their proficiency is essential for leading operational excellence. But all of those people capabilities start from a good and suitable hiring and integration.

The training process of a new employee in the organization and his professional integration exists on a wide spectrum of time ranges. However, an employee who leaves his job within the first year since recruitment constitutes a warning sign regarding the recruitment process (it could be a mistake in recruiting, the wrong person was recruited) or it could mean there is a problem in the process of integrating the employee in the organization—failed integration. In terms of costs, this is a wasteful event for the organization (the costs of the employee leaving the organization can be calculated according to the costs of recruiting and training.) As our understanding grow and go further into the depth of understanding operational excellence, we understand that recruiting, tracking, and training the right people for the work teams are crucial processes that will insure the team's future successes.

Sometimes operations may perceive as grey and routine area, however a range of professions, skills and qualifications such as: technologies, interpersonal, engineering and planning create a work environment that enables ongoing dynamic interaction of several fields under one roof. In addition, unlike organizations focused on specific occupations, work in the operations field allows the employees mobility and varied options for self development. Both to the length of the organization (in management positions) and to its width (moving between departments). This makes the operations work environment very dynamic and creates opportunities.

In light of that, one of the emphases in the employee recruitment process for positions in operations and one of the focuses for effective integration that promotes operational excellence is Diversity.

© Springer International Publishing Switzerland 2016
G. Issar, L.R. Navon, *Operational Excellence*, Management for Professionals,
DOI 10.1007/978-3-319-20699-8_11

11.1   Diversity in Operation

In management literature it is argued that the challenges within competitive, dynamic, and increasingly global markets (demanding innovation, creativity as well as flexibility) are best met by a broadened pool of experience and knowledge found in an effectively managed diverse workforce. Obviously, the innovative and creative potential inherent to a diverse workforce (in terms of gender, nationality, cultural background, religion, age, education, lifestyle, working style, way of thinking, etc.) can be used to bridge cultural boundaries and search for original problem solutions, innovative product ideas and targeted marketing initiatives. This diversity can become a competitive advantage (Pless & Maak, 2004).

Diversity management has to be built on solid normative grounds, on founding principles, understood as pillars of a culture of inclusion. Diversity is, first and foremost, a cultural question and thus a question of norms, values, beliefs and expectations. Given the fact that diversity is essentially about cultural norms and values, appropriate reflection work becomes a fundamental task to create a truly inclusive work environment where people from diverse backgrounds feel respected and recognized (Pless & Maak, 2004).

Therefore, diversity in the operations is critical to restore innovation, continuous improvement and leverage the organization competitiveness. In order to keep diversity in the organization, we need to have both very experienced people as well as people with less experience, while hiring, as well as gender, age diversity etc'. A diverse hiring for operations will create the desired talents and capabilities we need in the organization. Also we need to have the adequate degrees and different job descriptions. As experience in operations may be very specific according to the product and technology. For that we must build before hiring the map of skills, competences and expertise that we would like to see in a mature operation.

11.2   Hiring Phases

Good hiring process for operation starts with:

11.2.1 Sourcing

Identification of the right sources is critical factor for success. Sources differ for the different.

Managers candidates with managerial background from same industry, candidates with managerial background from other industries, internal candidates who gained enough experience and ready to grow.

Experienced Engineers candidates with engineering degree and experience from same industry, candidates with engineering degree and experience from other industries, internal candidates with hands-on experience who gained enough experience and ready to grow.

In-Experienced Engineers mostly candidates from the right schools. Important: healthy Operations organization MUST recruit in-experienced engineers, they bring fresh academy perspective, they will learn on the job, and they will become the future experienced engineers and managers of the team. Always allow 20–30 % of the new recruited people join with no significant experience, it pays!

Efficient sourcing is an HR<>Operation agreement on the preferred sources for all types of required new hires. Sources are defined by name: names of the schools, names of other companies in the industry, names of companies in other industries where the existing education and experience can bring value to your team.

11.2.2 Recruitment

Heaving a strong Sourcing mechanism in place ensures a continuous flow of good candidates into the recruitment pipe-line. Now it requires an efficient process of evaluating the qualities and potential of the candidates, with regards to the requirements of each and every open position.

In order to have the right candidates involves with several must—haves:

- High quality Job Description and Job Expectations document, solely defined and created by the hiring manager
- Professional HR team to manage the process and take part in sorting and screening the applications
- Internal hiring mechanism—critical for knowledge preserving and promoting opportunities for best employees.
- Evaluation methodology—interviews, skills exams, psychological exams etc.—any methodology agreed as the leading organization evaluation methodology.

Note: Leading global companies have realized that good hiring depends on how deep is the hiring manager's involvement in the process: the more managers and colleagues are involved in interviews and decision making, the highest probability for long and successful retention of the workforce exists. It is mostly advised that job offer is delivered to the candidate by the hiring manager, followed with cognates and open discussion on expectations and timeline.

11.3 NHO: New Hire Orientation

The NHO is one of the most important pillars of good start for a new hire. Usually, NHO is delivered to group of new hires on their first day in the new work place. Small organization may deliver the training and in introduction to a bunch of new employees that started on the last month or so, to ensure having a critical mass of people in the training. Typically, NHO will cover introduction of the history, vision and mission of the organization, org chart or structure, some fundamental cultural aspects or expectations, intro to the products or services of the company, followed by administrative, security and elementary safety requirements and IT guidelines or basic training. As these done, the new employees are usually taken to a guided tour, and meet senior manager who welcomes them on joining the team. This NHO usually takes the first day on board. Following this, new employees would go through particular training addressing their individual position.

The importance of such NHO process is in the equality of the start point for all employees, as well as in ensuring that critical safety requirements are delivered and eliminate any potential risk that new employees may face.

As mentioned earlier in this section, since Operation workforce is with high variety of expertise it is a good opportunity for new people to get to know other sections of the Operations team and meet people who will soon be their day to day partners (Fig. 11.1).

11.4 Tips to Managing Integration Process Which Is Effective for the Organization

Have you asked yourself which day employee's usually remembering best from their workplace?

Ask yourself and people around you and you will be surprised to discover that, in most cases, the first day at work is the one engraved in many employees memory. Regardless to which role they were recruited for, their position in the company and how much occupational experience they have come with. Usually employees remember in detail the experience of the first day at work, as though it happened yesterday.

Not for nothing is such a significant event. This is the employee's first meeting with the team with whom he will be working, with the colleagues in the organization whom he will meet on a regular basis and particularly this is a very significant experience of mutual first impression, The new employee creates a first impression, but the co-workers in the organization, the environment and atmosphere also create a first impression regarding him.

The goal of this section is to spread out option for several directions of thought and action, in order to insure a process management for the effective absorption and integration processes for the employees you recruit for your organization. Indeed the process of locating, sorting and recruiting candidates required considerable management and organizational efforts, what remains now, is to manage the absorption process and not wait for it to manage you.

Fig. 11.1 The hiring flow

An important guiding principle for an effective absorption process is to allocate time for learning, which includes reference to professional, social and cultural aspects. This time, if it is not defined, will be quickly becomes used for ongoing and immediate aspects. Therefore, it is important not to give up on the learning and, to be constantly accessible and available to the employee, to take an interest in him and answer his questions.

The reason for emphasizing this guiding principle is that management of an effective integration process enables quick absorption into the position, positive professional positioning and good social integration. These elements strengthen the connection between the employee and the workplace. The more established these elements become during the absorption period, the more they will affect the preservation of the employee in the organization.

11.4.1 The Ten Focus Points for Managing an Effective Absorption Process in the Organization

	Subject	Goal
1	Introduction meeting and defining expectations direct manager: employee	• In depth/thorough introduction/ acquaintance between manager and employee. • Setting/defining the expectations from the job (what does it include, what are the work interfaces, what is urgent, what are the challenges, what are the expectations from the employee, what are the expectations from the manager etc.) • Introduction with the role preparation program (contents- professional and personal skills, schedules, resources for learning) • Introduction to the organizational culture (what defines it? conduct in the company etc.)

(continued)

	Subject	Goal
2	Ongoing meetings manager: employee	• Tracking progress with the work program. • On the employee's side/hand- raising questions, requests for help, defining the methods and resources required to do the job, request for feedback.
3	Introductory talk with HR representative	• Referring the employee to a 1:1 meeting with the HR representative will allow him to learn (about) the organization, receive background regarding the organizational culture, the company's conduct and relevant contact people for questions regarding HR.
4	Building organizational networking by conducting introductory meetings with employees with whom work interfaces exist	• You, as a manager must map out the contact people in the organization that the employee will be working with throughout his role in the organization, and connect him to them. the purpose of the contacts are- – informal introduction in order to break the ice – creating a joint work infrastructure based on a trust relationship will promote teamwork in the future
5	Tour of the company- by the direct manager or team mate	• Introduction to the physical surroundings of the company (where everything is places, what logistics are required for certain services, who are the contact people)
6	Make sure the employee does not eat by himself during his first week in the organization	• This may sound basic but it turn out that this is something unnoticed by managers who are recruiting employees. the purpose of creating lunchtime company are- – To accelerate the integration of the employee in the team. – To learn about the company through "little stories"
7	Assigning a tutor that will accompany the employee during his first period in the organization	• An available and accessible answer/reply to general and social questions regarding the company. • Professional referrals to information sources and sharing knowledge. • Creating a safe and pleasant feeling in the new workplace. – NOTICE- it is important you prepare the tutor for the tutoring process and coordinate expectations with him before the recruiting the employee.
8	Shadowing	• Map out the events/employees that you would like the new worker to accompany. the purpose of shadowing- – Escorting a co-worker in order to learn

(continued)

	Subject	Goal
		the conduct in defined tasks, in the work day, in meetings, in the organizational work environment and in the professional conduct. – An opportunity to form informal contact/relationships and to study/learn the different people who work in the company and the effective way to integrate with them.
9	Participation in company meeting that are open to all the employees, or in meetings set/defined by you	• Learning the organizational culture and the decision making process • Exposure to key people in the company • Learning the business contents/ information?
10	Listen and ask questions	• You must be available and accessible to the employee and create in your meetings an environment that promotes his ability to ask questions and ask for help. At the same time, it is important that you ask questions and take an interest, mainly through listening, in order to builds a lasting trusting relationship with him

Reference

Pless, N., & Maak, T. (2004). Building an inclusive diversity culture: Principles, processes and practice. *Journal of Business Ethics, 54*, 129–147.

Human Resources (HR)   12

Although it seems that the contents of **HR** work has not changed along the years, actually over the last 20–30 years, the role of **HR** and their partnership with the business's operations has been continuously modified and transformed.

The question that needs to be asked is, whether the term 'resource for people' is still valid in information industries and for their employees? As nowadays every employee has knowledge based on "*Google*" search capabilities and people's independent skills do not require the same "*resource*" management as in the past.

The classic contents of **HR** support in the industrial business are composed of four major subjects, which need to be reviewed in regard to the new approaches:

1. Compensation and Benefits,
2. Learning and Development,
3. People's Performance and Management
4. Organizational Development.

12.1 Classic Approaches to Managing People in Technological Operations, Versus the New Approaches

The definition of people as a resource, was derived from a past perspective of system mechanisms. In advanced information based organizations it requires some adjustments. In the past people were valued mostly by their output power, similarly to machinery or energy, but in current industries people's important added value capabilities are in innovation and multi-disciplinary team integration, for example. These capabilities require a sophisticated approach, similar to the one required for the development and empowerment of people, which will be discussed in Chaps. 13 and 32.

One difference that distinguishes between people as a resource and physical resources, such as energy or capital equipment, is their relevance to the business operations success. While with physical resources, right timing, knowledge,

© Springer International Publishing Switzerland 2016   53
G. Issar, L.R. Navon, *Operational Excellence*, Management for Professionals,
DOI 10.1007/978-3-319-20699-8_12

experience and professional management should be enough in order to reach excellent operational and business results, with people management those capabilities are not enough.

In order to excel in work and in the management of employees, the professional manager needs to acquire "soft skills" and "emotional intelligence". These terms, in regard to the operations daily life, describe: role modeling, motivation, openness, listening and care for employees. Leaders and managers also need to empower their employees, provide guidance, and support and increase the employee's satisfaction, contribution and engagement. Several of these capabilities are discussed in specific chapters such as Chaps. 7, 24, 25 and 26.

Those skills are the most important technical and professional managerial skills.

> Unlike managing physical resources, empowering people and leading by example, require soft skills such as: listening, caring, role model, honesty and empathy.

12.2 Personal and Team Learning and Development

There is a significant difference between the focus that is put on two of HR's major responsibilities- compensation and performance management, and the focus put on the other two HR responsibilities- personal and team development. Focusing on the management does not leverage the huge potential, which exists in people's contribution to operational success, as much as focus on people's motivation and development. Sometime, due to mistakes in cost calculations, HR professionals focus more on compensation, benefits and performance management and invest less in people's personal and team development. Leveraging people's potential entirely changes the organization's operational and business results. Intensive work on people's personal development, together with teamwork and team development, will bring to a step function in all of the business's operational results.

Development of personal and team learning is the most exciting and rewarding work in the organization. Unfortunately, in some operations organizations, it is currently a dimension trend. People can gain significant knowledge capabilities through the web, and develop their ability in independent decision making. Teams have many new ways to connect socially, share information and through these electronics knowledge sharing systems, develop themselves to reach high professional and performance levels. The new web resourced knowledge and e-learning, leverage the people's and the team's professional development. The more the individual and the team invest in innovation, personal and team development, and the more personal and team professional development become a central steering engine for the business operation, the greater the breakthroughs, results and business wins that can happen in the operations.

Emotional intelligence, coaching, mentoring, inspiring and listening together with e-learning and team development, drive current operations performance to their best results.

Innovation in the Operations

13

Innovation is less frequently connected with the operations in industrial companies. Usually, innovation is expected from the Research and Development and design teams but less so from the operations people. However, as most of the company's budget is controlled and spent by the operations, if innovation is not promoted in operations, opportunities for improvement in costs and other major areas will be missed. Every quantum of innovation which brings a saving of 1 % to the operations budget, can be multiplied by the total sum of the company's budget, as large as it may be.

> The larger the company's budget is the larger the savings, in millions, that will flow as a result of innovation in the operations.

The first paradigm shift and the first form of thinking outside of the conventions that needs to proliferate throughout the company is the saving opportunity brought on by the innovations in the operations. Once innovation becomes a way of life in operations it will encourage innovation throughout the company. We can drive innovations in the operations by continuously seeking, exploring, renewing and improving the operations existing methodologies and by substituting expensive processes with new, lean and cost saving ones. It means continuously driving change in the organization. However, a change in the operations methodologies before it is properly ready can expose the operations to financial risks.

© Springer International Publishing Switzerland 2016
G. Issar, L.R. Navon, *Operational Excellence*, Management for Professionals,
DOI 10.1007/978-3-319-20699-8_13

13.1   Product Quality and Robustness as a Prerequisite for Innovation

Changes in processes should not be applied until after the operations and the product's *KPI's* for *quality*, *cost* and manufacturability have reached a relative degree of stability and consistency. Even then, innovative ideas or processes can be only implemented after they pass a structured and careful analysis by the *Control Change Board* (*CCB*). In order to receive a professional compression of the new recommended innovative process properly compared to the current one, a data driven statistical analysis and a compression needs to be applied by the initiating team and the management team. Furthermore, as described in Chap. 28, before any changes are implemented risk considerations and *return on investment* calculations need to take place. Once there has been a shift in the paradigm of *innovation in operation*, after the innovative changes have been implemented, quality and the reliability needs to be reviewed through a consistent performance and a structured system.

We use *KPI's* and *decision support systems* to verify that the critical parameters of the product's performance, at the customer's site, such as *yield*, *COG*, *cycle time*, reliability and other critical parameters, have an improvement trend. At this stage, the operations organization is mature enough to extend its *innovative* influence to nearby fields. *Innovation* can start with small steps, such as improvements in manufacturing routines, which can bring benefit through the reduction of *cycle time*, or improvement in the material yield or *utilization* improvements of the production machines.

After innovative improvements have been implemented in the product's costs such as yield, COGs and cycle time, then the *innovations* can be extended to improvements in the product's design parameters. Innovative improvement in the product's process and performance parameters lower the product's cost structure within the design configuration. Innovation in operations can reach the highest level by improving the product's performance at the customer's use as well as improving the product's production parameters in-house, in the operation.

> Do you know how many innovative improvement changes are implemented in the operations every week?

13.2   Notes for Promoting Innovation in the Operations

- There are many innovative people in the operations—technicians, engineers, managers, service people and industrial engineers. Innovation is not limited to certain graduates of certain faculties, or to a specific job, or level of experience. Innovation can come from a veteran technician or engineer as well as from someone who has recently graduated from college. An operations team member studies for an average of 3–5 years for his professional degree, while he spends tens of years at his workplace. Those years can be as rich with innovative improvements as his university days.

- When we establish a culture that expects innovation from every individual, in his area of responsibility, we will promote many innovative ideas.
- When we promote innovation in the operations, we get breakthrough ideas in all of the different disciplines of the operations: in technology, cost, people and organizational performances, in supply chain and manufacturing. These improvements significantly change in the product's COG.

A product can reach an improvement of between 20 % and 50 % in COG by leveraging the innovation of every individual in the operations.

13.3   How Professional Literature Defines Innovation?

Innovation: "the successful implementation of creative ideas by an organization" (Amabile, 1988). It consists of two major stages: the generation of new and useful ideas (creativity) and their implementation (West, 2002). An innovation can be considered new to an individual adopter, a group or team, an organization, an industry or the wider society (Gopalakrishnan & Damanpour, 1997; West & Farr, 1990). Innovation adoption is a means of creating change in the organization to ensure adaptive behavior and is intended to change the organization so that it maintains or improves its level of performance or effectiveness.

These days innovation is the engine of local and global economies. It promotes the competitiveness of the organizations in which it is developed, in part because it enables them to become flexible and provide an appropriate response to the changing demands of the market.

When we refer to innovation it is important to emphasize that innovation is not the solution but a way of organizational thinking and organizational thinking is dependent and derived from the organizational culture.

Many of the innovative ideas arrive while performing work or as a result of interactions between the workers, which is why innovation is a thing that can be managed. Researches have proven that inter organizational conditions are crucial factors in the encouragement of innovation among workers.

13.4   Factors that Influence Innovation Among Employees?

- Innovative strategies in the organization
- Organizational structure (bureaucratic/organizational flexibility)
- Organizational climate

- Team interactions (such as: organizational learning, communication between teams)
- The workers implementation capabilities
- Psychological conditions (such as: psychological safety/psychological meaning psychological availability) as described by Kahn's (1990) theory in Chap. 26.

> A leader, who has very strong impact on his workers behavior, has a crucial role in motivating them towards innovation.

When a successful leader simultaneously uses direct and indirect tactics to encourage innovation.

Innovative leaders have a vision that is motivated by values and "pulling" those who follow them to implement it. They are open to new and wide knowledge and information; they are always collecting knowledge, and manage to connect knowledge from different fields to the work processes they are operating. They are always learning and always searching for sources of knowledge and changes that are related to their area, they are open to changes around them, they have the ability to see the needs of others; they are inspiring; they empower those who follow them and believe in their ability to bring ideas by themselves.

From the systemic perspective, innovation refers to three general phases often referred to initiation (pre adoption decision), adoption (decision) and implementation (post-adoption) (Pierce and Delbecq, 1977; Rogers, 1995; Zmud, 1982):

13.5 General Phases in Innovation

- Phase 1—initiation
  Consists of activities that pertain to recognizing a need, searching for solutions, becoming aware of existing innovations, identifying suitable innovations and proposing some for adoption (Duncan, 1976; Rogers, 1995).
- Phase 2—adoption
  Organizations conduct activities within an environmental context—they obtain inputs from the environment, respond to its demands and offer their services or products to it. The external environment provides opportunities (information, resources, technology) and constraints (regulation, restriction on capital or information) (Damanpour & Schneider, 2006).
- Phase 3—Idea implementation
  As the habituation, organizational embedding and institutionalization of the novel idea in the system.
  An organization that wants to implement innovation needs to implement organizational programs which promote innovation, in order to carry it out. Adopting these programs sends out a message that innovation is an important thing to the

Fig. 13.1 The three general phases of innovation

organization. Which is why as an operations manager, it is important to decide (Fig. 13.1):

Which programs do you want to adopt or develop in order to promote innovation among your team?

References

Amabile, T. M. (1988). A model of creativity and innovation in organizations. *Research in Organizational Behavior, 10*, 123–167.

Damanpour, F., & Schneider, M. (2006). Phases of the adoption of innovation in organizations: Effects of environment, organization and top managers. *British Journal of Management, 17*, 215–236.

Duncan, R. B. (1976). The ambidextrous organization: Designing dual structures for innovation. In R. H. Kilmann, L. R. Pondy, & D. P. Slevin (Eds.), *The management of organizational design: Strategy implementation* (Vol. 1, pp. 167–188). New York: North-Holland.

Gopalakrishnan, S., & Damanpour, F. (1997). A review of innovation research in economics, sociology, and technology management. *Omega, 25*, 15–28.

Kahn, W. A. (1990). Psychological conditions of personal engagement and disengagement at work. *Academy of Management Journal, 33*(4), 692–724.

Pierce, J. L., & Delbecq, A. L. (1977). Organization structure, individual attitudes and innovation. *Academy of Management Review, 2*, 27–37.

Rogers, E. M. (1995). *Diffusion of innovations*. New York: Free Press.

West, M. A. (2002). Sparkling fountains or stagnant ponds: An integrative model of creativity and innovation implementation in work groups. *Applied Psychology: An International Review, 51*(3), 355–424.

West, M. A., & Farr, J. L. (1990). Innovation at work. In M. A. West & J. L. Farr (Eds.), *Innovation and creativity at work* (pp. 3–13). New York: Wiley.

Zmud, R. W. (1982). Diffusion of modern software practices: Influence of centralization and formalization. *Management Science, 28*, 1421–1431.

Interfaces and Their Improvement in Operations

14

Systematic thinking is a bird's—eye view, a wide observation of the organization and other organizations that are in working interfaces with them. Systematic observation examines and develops the connections between the departments (the visible and the invisible, the direct and the direct and indirect). *Systematic thought* processes also take into account hard components such as work indices and interdependence in the production process as well as soft components related to the organizational culture, characteristics of interpersonal communication, balance of power etc.

Best is to adopt work routines that will promote this systematic thinking and help leverage the operations processes, in order to manage, as well as decisions that promote the reaching of goals, as *AOS*, Cost reduction and other operations goals. The interfaces must be managed, they must not manage us. Therefore there is great importance to harness all of the parties involved in the task or interface.

Harnessing can be based on:

- Involvement in the preparations of work plans.
- Encouragement and use of ideas of the people involved in the interface.
- Knowing how to speak the professional language of the person, who conducts the correspondence with the interface? And furthermore, the ability to identify the characteristics of their interpersonal communication and how knowing to manage the interpersonal dynamics.
- To allow an atmosphere of openness and to be attentive and empathetic to all those involved in the interface.

One of the important components in management of work interfaces is constructive conflict management in the links where trouble in the "flow" exists. Every such conflict can delay reaching the joint goal, even if it was agreed upon during the structured work meetings. Which is why it is important to be aware, that different players in the interface may have different needs; To identify the needs of all of the involved in the interface in question; To think together of alternatives that will

© Springer International Publishing Switzerland 2016
G. Issar, L.R. Navon, *Operational Excellence*, Management for Professionals,
DOI 10.1007/978-3-319-20699-8_14

provide a mutual and appropriate solution to the needs that arise during the conflict; to reach the common solution out of mutual consent and commitment.

In conclusion, especially in this day and age of the complex global workspaces in which organizations exist there is a growing requirement to process more information, this affects the internal and external communication processes and makes reaching decisions more complex.

This requires leveraging the interpersonal interactions in the organization and efficient management of resources that will promote implementation of the decision making processes.

> Interface management (also called network structure) promotes collaboration between the different links of the chain, which is more beneficial for the organization than the benefits each link receives on its own.

Just in Time (JIT)

15

15.1 Planning Principles for Applying the JIT Methodology

There are many ways to control and manage the timing of material's arrival to the production floor. Each of the methodologies has its own benefits. One of the most effective and efficient ways to support assurance of supply, without risking high inventory levels, high storage cost and excess in work in process (WIP) is using the *Just in Time* methodology.

> **JIT** material management synchronizes the material and the parts arrival time with the exact date and time in which they are needed for production.

Using the **JIT** methodology for timing parts arrival demonstrates high levels of alignment between the parties within the operations. It requires alignment between the different departments during the preparation phase as well as continuous communication along the implementation process. The planning department needs to provide accurate mapping of the material requirements, and the exact time it is needed for the production. This list is important in order to meet the operations' commitments of product supply to the customers. Providing a list of the parts arrival schedules, makes it easy to extract, the daily or hourly material required by the production, from the overall 'material product tree' list. The scheduling of material's arrival also requires precise mapping of the material flow through the production floor. Some requirements are set based on the time that production starts and some are based on the time that production is scheduled to end. Figure 15.1 demonstrate scheduling of parts arrival according to production's start and according to the end of production.

© Springer International Publishing Switzerland 2016
G. Issar, L.R. Navon, *Operational Excellence*, Management for Professionals,
DOI 10.1007/978-3-319-20699-8_15

Fig. 15.1 Material flow
mapping

15.2   Supply Chain Practices in Applying JIT Methodology

In order to support the *JIT* material arrival and its management, when applying JIT
methodology the *Supply Chain* team has to make the necessary agreements with the
designated *JIT* vendors. Those agreements, need to address key elements, such as
the degree of freedom within the *JIT* timing.

For example: the production supply chain and the vendors need to align and
agree on the JIT material's arrival time and frequency.

They need to make it clear, and verify the time that the material will be supplied
along the day, whether it will be during the first or the second half of the day.

In certain cases the agreements even require specification of the exact hour of the
part's arrival.

This accurate supply system needs some flexibility in order to manage the
changes. For example, in periods when new products are introduced into the line
(see Chap. 23).

We always need to make sure that our JIT material planning system keeps the
material and production quality as well as Assurance of Supply as its highest
priority. That means that if a part or a material is rejected, due to lacking quality
or because it does not meet the specifications, the production plans will not be
disturbed as a result and the quality part replacing the rejected part will arrive Just
in Time.

A *JIT* communication method needs to be established and agreed upon externally, between the organization and its vendors, and internally between the production floor, warehouse and the supply chain. All of the parties, such as planning,
supply chain, production floor and vendor, need to know, every day, the exact parts
which are expected to arrive on that day.

Accurate and effective daily alignment of the *JIT* system, between all parties, is
mandatory in order to control any changes. When a new product is introduced and
launched, we need continuous updates from the vendors, due to the high frequency
of change in the parts specifications and the arrival due dates. If the vendors'
updating system fails to capture some of the changes, delays may be caused in
parts arrival time or parts will arrive on time but will not be according to the latest
revisions or improvements.

Since using the *JIT* methodology requires significant efforts, and in many cases
it's maintenance requires manual labor, it is not recommended for the majority of
the parts. We will usually prefer to have a good ratio between the effort required to
maintain the *JIT* timing and its cost benefits to the organization.

In order to be efficient and cost effective, we will usually choose to use the *JIT* methodology for the high value items. This practice supports the *operational excellence* objective to reduce excess *inventory*, as the cost of storage for large items is high and they are a constraint on exploiting storage room. In the case of sensitive materials, such as chemicals or very expensive critical items, the JIT methodology prevents their exposure to damages due to long storage periods.

The *JIT* practice is one of the most important systems who supports *AOS*, it does so by making the supply chain bottlenecks and the production line constraints more visible. When we keep the production floor clean of excess inventory, between the production start stations and up to the finished goods, we can easily identify the line constraint, by the increase of inventory before it. The vendor parts and processes, who are not robust enough, will also float up rapidly and will be distinguished from the rest due to their continuous deficiency. Naturally, the *JIT* methodology can be used for all items, not only for those with the highest value and the largest volume, as long as we make sure that the effort that goes into their maintenance is worthwhile.

Does the operations plan to receive a certain material just in time cause an AOS risk due to delays in material arrival from our vendors?

When we keep to the above rules for good JIT planning, management and communication, the *AOS* risk for those specific items is not increased. On the contrary, the same will happen when managing other parts by using the *JIT* method, the attention to their quality and cost will improve, as when managing special attention high value and high volume or critical items. An effective supply chain organization will usually use Vendor Managed Inventory (*VMI*) or 'Safety Stock' at supplier's site, to go hand in hand with the *JIT* timing. So both high *AOS* and low inventory and WIP and storage costs can be enjoyed.

Kanban

16

16.1 The Concept in Principals of the Kanban System

Kanban is a scheduling and physical supply system which ensures *Lean* and *just-in-time* production. With the Kanban system we control the logistic chain from the production end's point of view. The basic concept of the Kanban methodology is having two physical locations for each needed item. Each one of the locations is called drawer, or a Kanban. Once the first Kanban is consumed we replace it with the second Kanban. Since we always replenish the empty Kanban, which was used for the production, first, the flow of the material to the production line is continuous without stops.

There are two main principles that keep a good Kanban method continuously operating and performing well.

The first principal is continuous maintenance of the Kanban system and the second is its visual management. Maintenance of the system means that we always adjust the Kanban's size to the fluctuations in production volumes and proportionally make changes in its demands for material. The second principal is visual reporting and continuous management of the Kanban system stocks on hand, all the time, in order to identify and control the quantities of parts and material.

16.2 Continuous Maintenance of the Kanban System

How does continuous maintenance of the Kanban system promote item flow to the production floor?

When we need, for example, 10 items of a certain part per week, and our Kanban size is 1 week, the amount of parts in the Kanban system is defined as 7–15 units at any given time.

What will an increase in demand to 12 units per week, in the above example, cause?

© Springer International Publishing Switzerland 2016
G. Issar, L.R. Navon, *Operational Excellence*, Management for Professionals,
DOI 10.1007/978-3-319-20699-8_16

In such a situation, if we do not maintain the Kanban's size properly and proportionally, by changing the Kanban size to 12 units, the production team will pull 12 parts from the Kanban, according to their needs, which will consume the extra units due to the increase in their demand. Very soon, by the middle of the following week, we will face a shortage of parts for the production. An increase in demand by the production is not always driven by good news, such as solid demand or an increase in sales. Sometimes, production will increase the quantity of parts withdrawn from the Kanban due to rejects of parts that do not meet the quality inspection criteria in the production line. Continuous follow up on the Kanban withdraw pace reveals fluctuation in the rejects quantities. In cases where parts are rejected on the production floor we can eliminate production time waste by sorting the parts before they enter the Kanban drawer. By doing so we resume the supply of parts and the continuity to the line, while solving the discrepancy in quality and applying tests and solutions offline.

Maintenance of the Kanban's size is also a helpful tool when we rollover to new products or different revisions of a current product. When we introduce a new product, which is called rollover, we want to wear out the old product's inventory. Then we respectively adjust the Kanban's size to the increase in the new product's sales and to the decrease of the old materials.

In product rollover situations, there is a critical point which is called the 'point of no return'. At this point we cannot replenish the old product anymore. A daily follow up on the Kanban's status gives us the crucial understanding as to whether we have or have not reached the rollover point of no return.

A rule of thumb is, that in order to avoid shortage or excess of material, important information of inventory of parts from the old revision is required, while launching new product in order to minimize scrap and money loss.

16.3   Visual Management and Reporting of Kanban

The second principal in Kanban parts management is using visual inspection and reporting procedures. As the two Kanbans have a defined and dedicate place on the production floor, excess or shortage in inventory are immediately visible to all of the teams that operate the production floor. The Kanban drawers should always and consistently be 80–100 % full. If the first drawer is 80–100 % full, we can be confident that our supply status, on one end, and the demand, on the other end, are balanced and operating correctly. However when our Kanban level is less than 80 %, we are confronting a situation in which we have less material left than we have consumed for the production, this is called a material shortage situation. If all of the second drawers are full we might have a 'stop of production' situation which stops us from consuming the material. Many times, rapid detection of the parts status, through a short glance, is important and helpful to the occupied manager in the busy production floor. In such a case he can rapidly assess, and conclude, whether there is a material shortage situation, and he can immediately start to investigate its root cause and implement solutions. The visual reporting is also a very important tool for those who are part of the supply chain team but are not physically located on the production floor. For example when a certain part, from a particular vendor, is in the organization's attention and focus, we continuously need the urgent information regarding its stock size. In such a case, visual reporting helps all of the parties, vendors, buyers, managers and engineers, to be updated, on the part shortage situation, all of the time and to understand the advances in the implementation of the shortage solution according to the rate of consumption and replenishment. Inspite of the fact that they are not in present on the production floor.

Kanban reports must have clear definitions, with color codes that represent the Kanban's status.

For example: when a specific part's stocking is between 1.5 and 2 items in the Kanban, the status color will show green, which means that the amount of material is sufficient. If the stock of parts is between 0.5 and 1.5 items the color code will be yellow, which indicates that the stock is approaching a dangerous zone of material shortage. When we have less than one part in the drawer, the situation will be marked as red which calls for immediate action, in order to avoid a stop of the production. The definitions should vary between the different types of raw material and the different production sensitivities to risk of assurance of supply.

In summary, good implantation of the Kanban methodology is an effective tool to assure continuous flow of raw material to the production line. Also the Kanban system immediately alerts to shortages or excess of material, which raises the ability to identify the production line's constraints and helps start an immediate search for solutions and applying them.

Key Performances Indicators (KPI) 17

17.1 Defining of Operations KPIs

For many Operations managers, a day does not pass without reviewing tens of our performance indicators. However, as we defined in the Chap. 4, there are three principles to be followed, which are the rules of the Operations reporting system: *KPI* reports must be *Important, Accurate* and *Highly Used* by the operations team. Their targets and time period measures must correlate to key operations activities.

Decision Support Systems generate the reports, while dashboards use *KPI's*. The latter must be limited to calculations of only the *most important* parameters which can be *accurately* measured in a *statistically significant portion* of the product population, or process in the operations. *KPI*s that are either not significant, or not in the critical operations path, constitute a waste engineering and management time, creating redundant meetings, and occupying both planners and analysts with the solution of irrelevant problems.

KPI measurements needs to be *accurate* with their relevant reference units to compare with. Their targets and time period measures needs to correlate to operations key activities.

Since improving *Yield* results is a most common Operations performance parameter, let's examine the above principles when applied to this *KPI*. The first stage of the work necessary to increase the Yield is to carry out a defect Pareto analysis, in which we clearly distinguish and calculate the failure rates for different defects, each of which now becomes a new *KPI*. Clearly, calculating *KPI* defects that are not directly correlated with the defect phenomena will jeopardize and postpone yield improvement results.

Exactly the same attention must be paid to the accuracy of *KPI*s used to monitor equipment or process performance. In this case the situation is often more complex, as even a single piece of equipment may contain numerous operating parameters. Perhaps one of the most important tasks that both the Engineering and R&D groups are required to carry out during the process development stage is the identification of the *KPI's* and the sensitivity of the process to deviations. Not distinguishing

© Springer International Publishing Switzerland 2016
G. Issar, L.R. Navon, *Operational Excellence*, Management for Professionals,
DOI 10.1007/978-3-319-20699-8_17

precisely between quality and non-quality performances of production machines or processes wastes engineering time trouble shooting a wrongly identified or measured root cause.

The calculation of *KPI* goals to be achieved over time must be both accurate and realistic. For example, incoming material quality *KPI* accuracy can be debated by the vendor's perception. A critical part of managing the vendor relationship is the agreement reached between the organizations on the material *KPI*'s and their method of measurement. Failure to do so can affect quality improvement effectiveness.

In the same way, production cycle time may be challenged by the production team, and product performance deviations by may be challenged the designer. In these examples, an objective measurement such as the multi-observation survey (MOS) or third party analysis can be used in order to define acceptable *KPI* goals. While calculating *Inventory* we need accuracy in the counting of items prior to, during and after production, each of which is a Financial *KPI*. Monthly and quarterly financial reports can be very sensitive to inventory calculations and cycle time accuracy.

In cases where *KPI*s and *DSS* are not accurate enough operations may shift to wrong destinations and waste of time and resources trying to fix not the relevant problems root causes.

> For improving operation performance, measured KPIs, needs to be **critical**, **accurate** and **significant**.

17.2   The Excess *KPI* Trap

In the other end of few critical and accurate KPIs scale there is a situation of excess in *KPI*s. An excess in *KPI*s may also serve to camouflage the complicated deep root cause. Constantly measuring too many parameters causes ambiguity and ineffective use of operations resources. In such cases, important trends are hidden in the background of irrelevant data. Teams proudly present chart after chart of *KPI* data that show their industriousness and ability to meet goals, but do not move the performance Yield or Cost in the desired direction. There is a natural tendency to deal with surface issues as opposed to confronting the complicated deep root cause. Sometimes we encounter Operations teams which are reluctant to deal with such problems, and most of their indicators and parameters are shown as meeting targets. If the organization likes a color code, in such cases all *KPI*'s will show green, and if the organization prefers charts or tables, then indicators will usually meet the target line. Consistently meeting *KPI* goals may be an indication that their definition and characterization require a review for improvement or elimination.

17.3   The Different KPIs Groups

The critical significant parameter *KPI's* come from four major groups or families, the first of which is the critical product specification. These indicators reflect physical and chemical characteristics of the product technology. Over time, even when a product consists tens of thousands of parts, sorting and consolidation of the indicators will sum up to 20 or 30 truly critical ones.

> Product **critical specifications** are those that are critical for **customer use** and **product performance**.

The second group of *KPI's* is the production indicators. Here also, there might be hundreds of production steps that must be consolidated and placed in around ten critical buckets. Just as the first *KPI's* family is the product characteristics, the second family consists of the production process or assembly indicators, such as *quality* and *cycle time*.

The third *KPI's* family is the financial indicators, as *COGs, Gross Margin*, and *Inventory*. Finally, a fourth group of operations *KPI's* comes from the supply chain area of responsibilities. The first three sets of indicators envelop the product core specifications, characteristics, production and cost. The supply chain *KPI's* measure parts and material availability, and vendor performance in quality and on time goods delivery to our production floor. In addition, supply chain *KPI's* show the quality of the logistics involved in receiving and sending of the goods. The last *KPI* family is that of the product performance *KPI's* in the customer's hands and customer satisfaction from product performances.

17.4   Defining and Quantizing KPIs Goals Value

Once we have clearly established the necessary critical indicators that envelops the product, we can define their long term improvement goals. One way for defining these goals is to use a linear regression of the *KPI* chart with time. Part of operational excellence is continuous improvement. A linear regression is a mathematical expression of measured parameters continuously improving over time. The assumption is that product characteristics, process and production, and the financial indicators are improving linearly over time.

A fundamental requirement of continuous improvement reality is that every quarter has better performance than its previous quarter, and every year *KPI* results are better than previous year. In order to secure a continuous improvement the future indicator number can be marked on the raising or descending slope of the last quarter or the last year's record.

While aspiring to greater achievement, some *KPI's* such as Yield are often not linear with time and effort. For example, to increase the yield from 70 % to a goal of

80 %, requires a reduction of the defect rate from one unit in three to one unit in five. At 90 % yield the defect rate has dropped to one unit in ten, i.e. an improvement of 100 %! The amount of time and possibly capital required to achieve each 10 % improvement of Yield may differ significantly, and this must be taken into account in setting reasonable and achievable goals.

We might say that after improving for example yield from 70 % goal to 80 %, or even 98 %, we had reached the maximum of improvement and there is no meaning full goal any more.

However, even aspiring for a goal of 98.5 % or 99.7 % and increasing goals with increments of 0.2 % is important, serious and achievable. Continuously aspiring for incremental improvements in *KPI* goals, will prevent Operations performance from accepting only moderate results. High goals will drive quarter over quarter of incremental improvements which are the daily challenge of *operational excellence*.

> To reach high *KPI* goals, such as 99 % yield, we continuously drive for incremental improvement in the *KPI* by encouraging team innovations, and rewarding both managers and teams for goal dedication.

LEAN Operations

18

18.1 *LEAN* History

Since it first showed up in 1988, the word "LEAN" has become synonymous with the culture of Continuous Improvement. It is based on the principles of continuously working to improve *Quality*, Workflow procedures and most importantly, Empowerment of the workforce in regard to implementing these goals. The latter principle was perhaps the most revolutionary aspect of its introduction at the time.

The Toyota Corporation, which was the first to integrate *LEAN* fundamentals and philosophy, has become a platform and role model both for academic and industrial learning and understanding regarding the implementation of continuous improvement in an organization (Liker, 2004; Ohno & Bodek, 1988). Many books have since been written based on their experience including text books, training materials for teaching and consulting, and courses devoted to *LEAN* implementation. Over time, *LEAN* also constantly broadens its influence over different kind of organizations, and has been applied to many additional disciplines and operational connotations. These include *LEAN* Manufacturing, Lean Six Sigma, Healthcare, *LEAN* Management, Lean Services, and so on.

18.2 Lean Basic Philosophy

LEAN philosophy is that of constant, pro-active initiative toward the goals of cost reduction and increased product quality, through empowerment of the workforce in the process of creating improvements and reducing waste. It thereby results in a learning organization in which each and every employee, team and system strives to continuously improve its results. Continuous learning takes place through group discussion, and sharing common rules, which include shared principles of behavior and culture. Structured methodologies for group problem solving and continuous improvement give employees, at all levels of the organization, skills and new ways of thinking on how to improve their performance. Through reduction and removal

© Springer International Publishing Switzerland 2016   77
G. Issar, L.R. Navon, *Operational Excellence*, Management for Professionals,
DOI 10.1007/978-3-319-20699-8_18

of waste, cost is reduced, gross margin and quality increase, and value is added to the product from a customer perspective (Womack & Jones, 2003).

This perspective is in direct contrast to the narrow minded approach that cost may be reduced simply by workforce reduction. *LEAN* leverages employees work content and results through *innovation* and constantly improving the quality of their performance and their productivity. As a consequence of improved productivity, reduced waste of time and materials, cost reduction is instantaneously achieved.

Although people and organizations tend to understand *LEAN* philosophy and practice in different ways, as individuals we tend to implement *LEAN* thinking at our homes and personal life without defining it as LEAN. We are even not aware that we are practicing *LEAN* principles or tools. For example, the way in which we manage our morning schedule at home before going to work, while constantly focusing on our goal to be at work on time. We manage our activities in an attempt to achieve maximum efficiency in meeting all the tasks in our schedule.

In many other household routines and activities we also practice *LEAN* operations, such as minimizing waste and inventory, conserving household energy, or doing laundry and shopping by need and not by schedule. In Operations, adopting *LEAN* tools is only the first step in the path that leads to a fundamental change.

18.3   Lean Tools, Principles and Their Implementation

There are a number of *LEAN* tools to implement in every Operations group:

- *Kaizen* events for improving processes, such as production, supply chain logistics and warehouse, etc. (Masaaki, 2012).
- *5S* focusing on order and cleanliness on the production floor, laboratories and warehouses (Masaaki, 2012).
- VSM, Visual Management, and Poka Yoke on doing things right the first time.
- A3 methodology for problem solving and improvements.

All of these excellent innovative processes to effect change in behavior will drive performance improvement from both the quality and other Operations improvement aspects. But all these changes will not last long, without a fundamental change in our way of thinking to that of scientific *LEAN* thinking.

> With *LEAN* thinking, and implementation of the tools described, *LEAN* culture will become part of the organizations mode of thinking, and will have a lasting effect.

In their article in the Harvard Business Review: "Decoding the DNA of the Toyota production System", Bowen and Spears, describe four basic rules in learning of *LEAN* philosophy:

- All activities must be structured
- Customer-Supplier connections must be clear
- Path flows must be specific and simple

Improvement must be accomplished through experimentation in a scientific manner at all levels of the organization.

Behind the rules given above are a wide range of behaviors which help the organization to establish a common, shared mode of operation. People develop language to design and improve systems, in which even the most basic set of activities, either manual or automatic, is a system. We need to dig deeply under our routine modes of thought and strive to reach the fundamentals of our operational philosophy. The roots of LEAN thinking are found under the layer of the rules of implementation. Once we had reached this layer, the next step for implementation will be straight forward.

There are five basic principles for *LEAN* implementation (Flinchbaugh & Carlino, 2005) in operations:

- Principle #1—Direct Observation.

  Observation should be carried out as close as possible to the place in which activities are performed, without the presence of filters. This practice is the key to understanding the current reality and defining the correct steps for learning and improvement.
- Principle #2—Systematic Waste Elimination.

  The key practice for systematic waste elimination is to challenge current assumptions, thereby acquiring a fresh view of the world through "new lenses". This manner of observation enables us to identify waste on the fly, and with time we do not tolerate wasted material, time, or activity. By systematically reducing waste, in a step by step manner we approach a more *LEAN* work environment.
- Principle #3—Establishing a High Level of Agreement on What and How.

  This key principle tackles major pitfalls in the implementation of *Lean* thinking; the process of impacting people's behaviors while achieving agreement on what to improve, and how to improve them. It also contains a second part which is more technical and related to all the techniques and tools enabling the workforce to perform work as it should be done (i.e. Work Instructions, Checklists, Diagrams, etc.)
- Principle #4—Systematic Problem Solving.

  Systematic problem solving's importance lies in its goal to reach the true root cause of a problematic event and eliminate its repetition. In addition, the message beyond the requirement to introduce systematic problem solving is that each and every employee can and should practice such problem solving at every level of their activities. On this point, a paradigm shift is needed, as people are generally skeptical about this rule's applicability and their own problem solving capabilities. However, there are many case studies by *LEAN* experts who have shown that problem solving practices taught across the organization have succeeded with worthwhile results.

Problems that remain unsolved grow more complicated with time, and can become a hundred times more difficult for solution. Use of the four *LEAN* principles of *observation, waste elimination, improvements and problem solving* consistently over time eliminates issues, and prevents their further growth into larger problems.

For example, a quality problem that was identified in the development lab will be ten times more complicated to solve on the production floor and a hundred times more complicated to solve at customer's sites after tens of product units were released. The motivation to eliminate and continuously solve issues at the lowest level of the organization is shown in the attached scheme of Fig. 18.1.

- Principal #5—Creating a *Learning Organization*.

As we have said at the start of this chapter, *Learning* is mostly what *LEAN* is all about. Learning is the way to create change while being willing to improve Quality or Performance. Kaizen, as a "change for good" philosophy, is based on individuals and the organization learning from both their successes and failures. The correct implementation of LEAN thinking constantly turns the wheel of improvement through a continuous learning process at all levels. Eventually, 'Learners' will become teachers who will then become leaders.

The role of leaders, and the quality of their leadership in driving and implementing change is critical, because *LEAN* is all about change in the organization, the way we perform, think and behave. Without the strong support and example of senior management, it simply won't gain acceptance and constant use. *LEAN* bibliography includes many aspects and examples of *LEAN* leadership.

As *LEAN* connects all employees in the organization, successfully driving *LEAN* needs to include all employees as part of the change. Every employee who teaches or coaches a colleague for *LEAN* improvement simultaneously

Fig. 18.1 Problems complexity increases if not solving them at the lowest operations level in a *LEAN* way

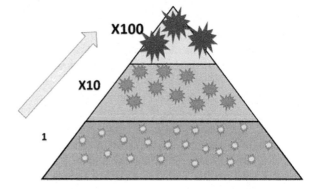

develops their own leadership in Operations. Leaders must be Teachers and Learners. It is a crucial part of the continuous improvement mindset.

Adopting *LEAN* principles and thinking in every part of our daily work will significantly advance our organization, as *LEAN* tools and techniques become an integral part of our progress.

References

Flinchbaugh, J., & Carlino, A. (2005). *The Hitchhiker's guide to lean: Lessons from the road.* Dearborn, MI: SME.

Liker, J. (2004). *The Toyota way: 14 Management principles from the World's greatest manufacturer.* New York: McGraw-Hill.

Masaaki, I. (2012). *Gemba Kaizen: A commonsense approach to a continuous improvement strategy.* New York: McGraw-Hill.

Ohno, T., & Bodek, N. (1988). *Toyota production system: Beyond large scale production.* Parker, CO: BookCrafters.

Womack, J., & Jones, D. (2003). *Lean thinking: Banish waste and create wealth in your corporation.* New York: Simon & Schuster.

Leadership in the Operations

19

19.1 The Ways for Building Leadership in the Operations

Many times, managers who have just joined the operations ask how they should build their leadership in the operations world. As in many other disciplines, leadership can be built through using the shorter way, utilizing one's managerial authorization or through long term professional building of managerial credibility.

> The longer way to build leadership in the operations is by constantly and continuously bringing the operations teams to results which have added value.

By taking the longer route, reaching *operational excellence* by continuously bringing quality results, the operations leader gains his team's trust and respect and consequently gains their commitment.

Building leadership in operations usually requires several years of journeying through the operations world.

During those years, while learnings the operations practices, the operations leader encounters technologies, products and production sites as well as different organizational cultures in the different operations departments.

By successfully experiencing the diversity and complexity of the operations in the operation's business environment, the new leader learns how to reach the different departments specific goals. Furthermore, after experiencing the unique contribution of every department, such as supply chain, engineering, manufacturing or planning, we learn how to leverage their specific strengths and how to integrate them into the operations mutual goals, such as assurance of supply (AOS), quality and Gross Margin improvements.

© Springer International Publishing Switzerland 2016
G. Issar, L.R. Navon, *Operational Excellence*, Management for Professionals,
DOI 10.1007/978-3-319-20699-8_19

> Building operations leadership is done by gaining the trust and commitment of the people in the different operations disciplines as well as through personal experience and consistent quality results.

The challenge that arises while gaining the required experience in operations is, that in operations a month of good results can always turnaround into a month, or even a sequential quarter, of bad results. Situations of short terms success are prevented by building a culture and infrastructure of *operational excellence* in operations. Operations leadership results are based and built on delivering continuous and consistent good results. A representing phrase often used in the operations is 'bringing *Day in and day out* results throughout the year'.

The ultimate answer for the frequently asked question, how to build successful leadership in operations? Is:

> Reaching continues and consistent good results, with a minimum of surprises in output, quality or costs.

Examples for surprises in the operations are: unexpected technical or technological failures, limitations on supply of the demand, not meeting assurance of supply, as well as significant quality issues or unpredicted financial losses due to scrap or missing material in the cycle count. Successful leadership goals are apparent in well-defined and clear consistent operation. Yet there are some challenges to overcome.

> The leadership's challenge in operations is, to minimize the appearance of unpredicted hits in performances due to the statistical nature and variability of the operations.

19.2 Operations Leadership and Leveraging the Coordination Between the Departments

The answer for continuous and consistent good results in operations is built in the multi-disciplinary departmental structure. Excellent coordination and simultaneous operation between the different departments, controls and reduces the statistical nature and the variance in operations. Coordination between the departments also proactively prevents and buffers major unexpected drops and misses due to unexpected events.

The analogy often used for operations who perform is well is an excellent orchestra. However, there is a difference in this analogy. While for a well performing orchestra the playground is the concert hall, which is concrete and stable. The operations orchestra's playground resembles a raft rising and falling in the waves of the business environment's turbulent sea. Daily and weekly coordination and integration between Manufacturing, Engineering, Planning, Supply Chain and Services reduces the variability and the unpredicted failures.

For example: preventing production stops in manufacturing can be achieved through excellent coordination between the vendor, the supply chain and engineering. Upcoming supply risks which are known in advance may be prevented through suitable solutions coordinated by the above mentioned parties. The same applies to unpredicted quality failure events or financial misses. A leadership which foresees the rising of risks and prevents their occurrence, by coordinating between the different operations departments, will be recognized and accepted as thorough leadership.

> Operations leadership that drives cooperation and integration between departments, in order to prevent occurrence of failures, achieves excellence which motivates further and new integrations.

19.3   The Ways for Learning of Operations Leadership

Often, the potential for reaching operational excellence is not materialized due to lack in motivation to implement changes or due to lack of interest in raising the results above their performance of 90 %. In some organizations the will to drive for excellence exists but there is a lack in experience, regarding how to reach high performance yields or low costs or technical innovation. The question frequently asked is how to bridge the gap in the management's experience in operations excellence?

Usually the operations leaders have experience in managing one or two of the disciplines in the operations and do not have detailed knowledge and experience in the other five disciplines; Manufacturing, engineering, supply chain, planning and services. A background in only two of the five disciplines can prevent the organization from reaching a level of excellence within short time frame. Especially as leveraging integration between the departments yields significant cost saving benefits and efficiency gains. The solution for this gap can come from several directions. One way is by planning the development of operations leaders ahead of time, by acquiring the knowledge and a substantial managerial period in three of the five disciplines. This can be achieved through job rotations between the different operations department managers.

A second solution is to consult with and be mentored by internal or external, experienced, operations managers who have already reached operational excellence and who can guide the new leaders on how to reach the operational excellence goals. In both ways, reaching operational excellence is achieved by meeting above

90 % of the business's operations goals. These high results are achieved through and while building leadership, during a long term of very good and consistent achievements. It is a long but safe way for the leader to reach a satisfying and joyful career as well as gain enthusiastic and satisfied employees.

Meetings and LEAN Decision Making 20

20.1 Effective Meeting Versus Effective Meeting and Meetings with Added Value

Although meetings are the most effective organizational communication structure for fruitful discussions, knowledge sharing and decision making, if the operations people do not strive to make every meeting yield action items and results, the meeting may become time and resource consuming. In other words instead of a being a leverage tool for execution, a meeting can transform into a burden on activities and on execution. In every operations meeting, weekly, monthly or quarterly, objectives and *KPI* need to continuously rise above their existing level of performance, otherwise the meetings will not be effective, and well known knowledge and results will be replicated.

There are many technical recommendations for holding effective meetings. Setting and keeping an agenda, starting the meeting with a defined expected outcome, having a meeting chairman, having a meeting' time keeper' as well as several more recommendations. All of these recommendations are very important and are useful for holding effective meetings. However, although some of these procedures are common practices in the organization, those meetings results are not always tangible and do not always improve the operations performance. Sometimes forums do not focus on results and execution, and prefer detailed discussions which do not have clear operative directions. The meeting leader may impose an appearance of using all the technicalities of an effective meeting, but the core of the meeting, the important and significant added value results, might not exist. When we join a meeting or, are in charge of one, we need to ask ourselves, what are the core and long term applicable results of the discussion?

© Springer International Publishing Switzerland 2016
G. Issar, L.R. Navon, *Operational Excellence*, Management for Professionals,
DOI 10.1007/978-3-319-20699-8_20

We should attend meetings after thinking about expected outcome of the meeting, and its contribution to the improvement of operations performance.
Ask yourself?
Which of meetings' outcomes, if implemented in my department, will drive measurable improvements?
Meeting discussion that a month later does not yield measurable improvement in the operations **KPI**s are not effective.

We need to set a high bar regarding our role in the meeting, and have *LEAN* philosophy and *operational excellence* on our mind. In order to have a reference point for quality meeting results, we can compare every meeting we attend to a meeting whose outcome decisions became, later on, a turning point in the improvement of operations performance.

For example, a yield improvement meeting that significantly changed yield results. A cost saving discussion that brought to a breakthrough in savings, or a quality discussion whose results drove quality performance improvement. In all of those breakthrough meetings, a process or methodology was changed or developed. Similar breakthroughs are potentially hidden in almost every operative meeting.

Once we have a 'breakthrough meeting' a previous turning point meeting, as a reference point in our mind, we can compare it to every meeting we attend. There are also some less technical and more cultural attitudes that will drive change in the meetings' effectiveness. For example, while attending or preparing an engineering or technology discussion, the discussion needs to be structured in a logical, known format in order to ease the meetings' attendees' flow of thought.

20.2 Using a Problem Solving Format in Order to Achieve an Effective Meeting

Using a *problem solving* format in meetings is always helpful for effective discussions in operations. The structured problem solving format helps everyone, in the meeting, stick to the same stage of the discussion. By having everyone on the same page all the time, the discussion advances in one direction and does not intuitively flow towards non-effective discussions and does not go backwards to its starting point. Furthermore, when we adhere to a problem solving format, we prevent jumping back and forth from the problem statement discussion, to the results phase or to the recommended solutions discussion.

The participants, of the meetings, role is very clear, during every step of the problem solving flow. In the 'discussion of the problem statement' stage, the participant's role is, to contribute by summarizing and phrasing the problem statement. When searching for the possible root cause the role of the meetings' members is to brainstorm and try to find the technical or technological reasons for

Fig. 20.1 Fish bone diagram for possible root cause brainstorm

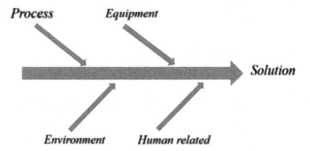

the situation. This structured and orderly way of thinking is important in order to fulfill one logical step before starting the next one.

Figure 20.1 describes possible root causes. The principal drawing is in a fish bone shape, in order to capture different root causes according to their families, process, equipment, environment and human relativity.

In technical discussions adopting structured process such as the 'seven steps of problem solving' increases meetings' effectiveness.

The seven steps for problem solving are:

1. Problem Statement,
2. Current Status,
3. Possible Root Cause,
4. Solutions Development,
5. Solution Testing,
6. Solution Implementation,
7. Documentation and periodical Check of Results.

Notes and recommendations, regarding the saving in time brought by use of problem solving for structured discussion.

Sometimes when a meetings' participants are very confident in themselves, and in their ability to solve the problem rapidly, they may skip the systematic problem solving process. Usually in such cases, after a few weeks the meeting goes back to square one and to day one, when the event started. By then, after several days have passed, records and data are missing, and the ones that were documented or stored are partial, and cannot correlate and support the hypothesis for the solution. In such cases a huge amount of work is needed in order to start the problem solving from the beginning. This waste of resources can usually be avoided by reaching a team decision, to always apply structured problem solving methods in technical meetings, even in cases that seem very easy to solve. A structured problem solving discussion never take more of the forums' time, than an unstructured intuitive one.

20.3   Data Driven Discussions and Ownership of Meeting Results

Another important element for creating meeting value and effectiveness, is having the discussion based purely on data. When we start our meeting *with the end in mind*, we need to define the owner of the discussed topic, from one of the operations departments or one of the different disciplines. The subjects' owner needs to present the subject and own the discussions' *KPI* and measurements, for upcoming meetings, for the next quarter and end of the year results.

Whether the subject is yield, material quality, parts or technology, it always needs to be discussed according to its *KPI* performance. It always helps to see the annual and quarterly charts of the discussed subject. Charts help the meetings' participant focus on the discussed subjects' monthly or quarterly trends. Major questions get answered immediately and intuitively.

For example: are quality indicators, cost saving results or customer satisfactions' *KPI* trends, down?

Is their *KPI* performance consistent and stable?

Does the *KPI* performance have high fluctuation with high standard deviation?

Or, is the indicator trend stable over time?

Once the topic has been captured in a dashboard format, with color coding of the current status, and the data shows the measured subjects' pattern in a chart, the sharing of knowledge in the meeting is very fast and efficient. The next step, brainstorming discussions, also goes fast, so the whole decision making discussion can take less than an hour, even when the discussions are in regard to complicated operational dilemmas. If data is properly collected and prepared, the ownership of the solution is clear, and the three parts of the meeting: sharing knowledge, team brainstorming and decision making, are structured, the meeting will be high quality. When a meeting is very effective and very short, it allows people to return to their work quickly and bring the solutions effectively. This is the lean way and culture, to have professional operation meetings and decision making.

Once an effective and value adding meeting's culture is achieved, people will appreciate their time saving and they will be ambassador for structured and value meetings.

Manufacturing Overhead (MOH) and Departmental Expense Control

21

In addition to the operations financial responsibility for the *Cost of Goods (COGs)*, *Bill of Material (BOM)*, labor costs, logistics and depreciations, operations are also responsible for the cost of their own activities, which are defined and calculated as *Manufacturing Overhead (MOH)*.

The **MOH** includes the operations costs for all of the indirect activities regarding the manufacturing of the product.

21.1 Practices for the Control of Manufacturing Overhead

There are a few 'hands on' practices for effective control of the **MOH**.

- First practice is to ensure that all of the operations departments own their monthly expenses control.
- Second practice is continuous reduction in the departmental costs in proportion to the product revenue.
- Third practice is *Innovation* and continuous improvement in departmental costs for **MOH** reduction

21.2 Department's Ownership of Their Monthly Expenses Control

Every operations department has to have its own goal for an annual spending and savings budget. The department's annual budget should be divided into monthly target numbers. Every departmental expenditure is attached to a saving budget tag and the system's saving owner is defined. The department's monthly spending pace is controlled on a weekly basis and before making any major decisions regarding expenses. In operations cost savings forums and meetings, the owners periodically report the monthly and quarterly saving goal achievements as opposed to the plans.

© Springer International Publishing Switzerland 2016
G. Issar, L.R. Navon, *Operational Excellence*, Management for Professionals,
DOI 10.1007/978-3-319-20699-8_21

Using the weekly, monthly and quarterly expense and saving control systems, will keep the *MOH* within the planned budget.

21.3   Department's Size in Relation to Product Output and Company Revenue

While the product ramp goes up and the amount of activities increases, there is tendency to increase the department's head count without noticing. This quickly results in a total operations increase in salaries, a rise in departmental expenses and consequently in an increase of the *MOH*. The same thing usually happens when the product's ramp goes down and there is need for MOH adjustments. We can debate whether it is possible for production to grow by factors while engineering and other indirect headcounts stay constant and low. There are a few opportunities and some recommended *Operational excellence* practices designed to achieve this. Herewith are some of the opportunities, previously reviewed in different chapters, which promote effectiveness and prevent over hiring for ramp.

Most of the best practices increase the operations efficiency and reduce the indirect headcount.

- Increase of effectiveness and reduction in the number of meetings, as described in the 'meetings' section.
- *LEAN* and precise *Decision Support Systems* and *KPI*. Reduction of the extra head count which supports activities with no added value.
- Increase of the production processes and the production tools strength, as well as significant reduction in the amount of task forces needed.
- Quality *NPI* process, launching a configurations with minimal changes in order to prevent over head counts in ramp.
- Increase in automation and consistency of the processes.

There are many more 'hands on' recommendations for increasing effectiveness and preventing extra head count. A good question to ask before every hiring process is, whether hiring is due to an increase in added value activities or due to troubleshooting of non-quality and non -added value situations.

In the latter case it is better to resolve the root cause of the non-quality situation while saving scrap, reducing costs and preventing extra hiring which increases the *MOH*.

Product ramp should improve the MOH revenue proportions. Improving meetings, *decision support systems* and effective *KPI*s and *NPI* will prevent extra hiring.

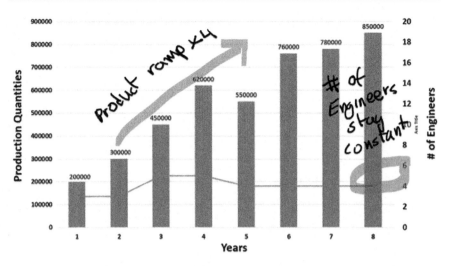

Fig. 21.1 Steady MOH cost following innovation activities

21.4   Innovation Is a Major Step Function Towards Decreasing the Department's Costs

The main opportunity to decrease operational costs is through *innovation*.

Innovation has an important role as a multiplier and enabler for improvement of processes and head count savings.

Example: Fig. 21.1, the chart describes a situation of production increasing by four times while the engineering head count remains steady, due to *innovations*.

Innovations are achieved by leveraging and encouraging engineers to pursue cost reducing projects as well as improving process automation and production strength. All of these activities reduce engineering's and production's head count, while production volume may double and triple.

> Significant stabilizing, simplifying and automating production processes keeps **MOH** steady while production grows by two to four times.

Manufacturing Excellence in Daily life

22

22.1 Practices for Implementations of Operation Excellence Tools in Manufacturing Daily Life

We assume that by now the reader accepts many of the operational excellence concepts and recommendations, however, he probably asks himself how to apply them in the manufacturing hectic reality and his operations daily life. Intuitively it is easy to agree for every method and tool importance and success by its own, the question is usually how can we coordinate between the different described methods and priorities that many times contradicts one the other?

The answer cannot come only through prioritization between different operations top activities. For example, we know that *AOS* is our first priority, but fortunately we should have urgent *NPI* tasks to complete at the same day as well, usually *NPI*s activities and *AOS* competes on same resources. Another frequent example is around cost saving activities. Usually we have to cut activities for cost saving in order to improve our *Gross Margin*, though in parallel we need to invest same resources in *quality* improvement projects.

Needless to say that *people motivation and development* activities by definition compete on people time and with the department's immediate output and deliverables tasks and resources. Many times we find ourselves pushing out *training* and *people development* for some weeks due to *AOS, NPI, COST* and Quality urgent activities. After we had prioritized our activities according to their urgency and importance, tactical and strategic, we still have the conflict in our daily decisions how to combine them all?

How do we implement the operational excellence recommendations in our daily life?

There are four recommended practices that helps to allocate a minimal though significant of manufacturing people time and resources, to activities that are not urgent as the *AOS, NPI,* and *Quality* daily tasks.

Example for not so urgent activities that we need merge in to our important and urgent activities are: people training and development, investment in infrastructure

© Springer International Publishing Switzerland 2016
G. Issar, L.R. Navon, *Operational Excellence*, Management for Professionals,
DOI 10.1007/978-3-319-20699-8_22

and technology, or in long term improvement project of safety, quality or other *innovations*.

> The four recommended practices are:
>
> Unite together of high priority and important activities.
> Small steps of implementation important but not urgent activities.
> Consistency of routines with long term action plans for people and development, team build and other not urgent activities.
> Continuity in implementing the plans of the important and value activities along years.

If we strive seriously and intentionally for excellence implementation, we will find many opportunity for applying those four practices combining between urgent and long term investment in important subjects.

22.2 Unite of Different Improvement Tasks and Activities

By *unite* activities we mean that we can combine an urgent task as *AOS* or *NPI* and use same resource for both at the same time. At a first glance people will reject sharing their resources with another activity. With the time, the process of evaluating resource sharing becomes a habit and culture, and will expose many opportunities for sharing. For example: joining some of *AOS*, *quality safety* or *NPI* tests on same testing equipment with same technicians and engineer. Not necessarily all software or chemicals or mechanics modules are connected in the product or at the production plant. Many times we can *unite* and test or work on single systems in parallel on different subjects.

22.3 Implementations of Significant Improvement Through Small Steps Practice

Second recommended practice is using *Small Steps* for the important but not urgent operations subject implementation. By practicing *small steps* we can invest between 15 and 30 min a day in precise focused activity and drive a break through with minimal investment of time. Examples for minimal dosage of time investment in daily activities are numerous:

- Ten minutes a week of *Safety Management by Walking Around* will drive safety to excellence but will not hurt *AOS* or *NPI* daily duties.
- Same practice works for *quality audits* of half an hour a week. Through using *small steps*, we can audit every week different system. It can be through auditing

product or production documentation and specifications accuracy in one occasion, and people process knowledge in the other week. Audit can be on quality systems accuracy, five S cleanliness and orderliness of the production floor, measurement tools accuracy, and calibration tools due dates and many other opportunities for improvements by *small steps*.

- People knowledge on lessons learn for preventing quality failure events to repeat can take place in a quick test in a stand up meeting on the production floor for 10–15 min a week.
- People development and innovation projects can reviewed for half an hour a month. Though half an hour is small step and is minimal time consumption but it can drive un-limited benefit for improvements in every subject through innovations as described in Chap. 13.

22.4 Practicing Changes Continuously and Consistently

When we come to implement changes in our schedule, our daily routine from one hand and the urgent priorities and tasks from the other hand are major resistant's to our intention for change implementation. Usually we can compete with *AOS* or *NPI* urgency, but through applying the four practices of *Unite* efforts in *Small Steps continuously* and *consistently* we create a window for change in a loaded schedule. Since manufacturing is relatively large and dynamic organization with several weekly urgent tasks, changes should not implement as a one timer, an instant activity, or as only short term solution. The *Unite, Small Steps, consistency* and *continuity* protects and helps changes to last for longer periods and even for years. Through assimilation of a more "holistic" philosophy, applying variety of practices in small steps, we can introduce changes in to the operations dynamic and multi priority production floor routine. Introducing important value subjects as people development and strategic improvements, enable us more control on our operations long term priorities and less acceptance to fire-fighting mode of operations. Investing in those long term valued activities, support crispiness and multitasking of the team. There is a common belief in manufacturing that, investing in peripheral important activities consumes people time and attentions from their core job. Actually, investing in long term quality improvements or people development, will free more of the manufacturing people time to contribute even more in their core tasks as *AOS*, *Cost* reduction and *Quality*.

When we invest in small quantities every day consistently in manufacturing value subjects as safety, quality, people development and innovation. Not only that it brings un-limited ROI in those fields but with time it improves the urgent subjects result as well.

New Product Introduction (NPI)

23

The transfer of a project from design schemes and formulations in research and development centers and laboratories to a functioning product is an exciting and critical organizational challenge. Coordination of its successful production with the Operations Group, and with the Marketing Group for its launch to the market is an opportunity for the organization to excel both *internally* and *externally*.

Improving effectiveness *internally* involves improving the communications and the accuracy of the information exchanged during product delivery between the developers and operations. Transfer product from design schemes and formulations to a functioning product is exciting challenge to excel in internal effectiveness. Development and operations teams well trained in using problem- solving methodologies such as the seven Steps, are an integral part of a strategy to improve internal technology transfer effectiveness.

Improved performance *externally* is directly related to the company's interaction with its customer. This begins with Marketing's choice of the customers who receive the first products. Inevitably, there are needs to over-come debugging and some "childhood problems". The suitability of the customer to take part in this excellent operational improvement opportunity, as well as the extent to which the customer is representative of others in the target market is a critical decision that influences successful product introduction. Once the product is in the hands of customers, a team headed by marketing and comprised of representatives of development, operations, and service closely follows the customer's experience. The team must quickly respond and solve customer complaints to a customer's maximum satisfaction from the new launched product, all the while generating feedback and "lessons learned" for their respective groups and upper management.

> Ask yourself whether Research and Development together with the operations team in your organization shares joint ownership and maximize coordination for NPI success?

© Springer International Publishing Switzerland 2016

G. Issar, L.R. Navon, *Operational Excellence*, Management for Professionals,
DOI 10.1007/978-3-319-20699-8_23

23.1 Timing of New Product Introduction

Major complexity and dilemma of *New Product Introductions,* is the product level
of maturity when product is released. On the one hand, delaying the full introduction during the Ramp stage (Fig. 23.1) allows for large scale statistical feedback in
terms of both manufacturing quality and cost. Most importantly, it provides customer reaction results and the time to debug possible complaints. However, these
benefits come at the price of placing the Time to Market window at greater risk
from competition and the possible loss of market share. On the other hand, an
ambitious development period combined with a short *Time to Market,* e.g. without
enabling field tests, can cause a company to introduce a premature product, with all
of the consequences that follow. Negative customer experience and lack of satisfaction can damage a product's reputation to the point that even expensive fixes
later on cannot undo the poor first impression. Under the best of circumstances, the
company's Gross Margin will suffer due to the extended cost load induced by the
need to fix early "teething" problems.

Note: The above debate is not relevant to the aviation or pharmaceutical
operations were product released is strictly after 100 % testing and validations.

One of the methodologies used to balance the two above described scenarios is
the use of **Key Performance Indicators** to track manufacturing and customer
reaction during the **NPI** launch period. These indicators help guide management
decision-making while navigating the launch:

- Two Financial KPIs, **COGs** and *Gross Margin*, are used to estimate the product
  maturity level—Introduction of an immature product will be reflected by
  increase of the product **COGS** and a quarterly *Gross Margin* decrease. Closely

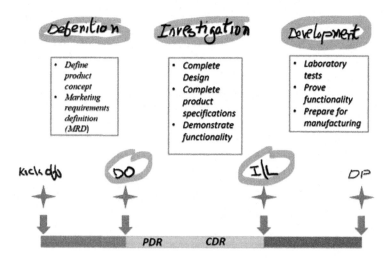

Fig. 23.1 Major product development stages their flow, content and documentation for each stage

monitoring these indicators will provide the first indications of risk due to immature NPI

- Customer Services and assurance KPIs can estimate customer satisfaction and indicate trends regarding urgent needs, in order not to delay *NPI* from reaching market. Also monthly and quarterly sales numbers and market share will reflect whether the competition has any leverage on market share due to an *NPI* delay.

In summary, managing the conflict of *New Product Introduction* launch timing can be controlled operatively by two boundaries. Too early introduction can be prevented through not exceeding significantly **BOM**, **COG**s and *Gross Margin* versus plan. Delay of *NPI* can be controlled through monitoring carefully customer satisfactions and monthly sales.

23.2   Structured Methodologies for Successful New Product Introduction and Release to the Market

For optimal *NPI* process several hand shake methodologies between developers and operations are practiced.

One of the methodologies for a quality hand shake between operations and R&D, is to add a small team from the engineering group to the R&D project at the Investigation stage of the development. The team input to the project on subjects such as engineering technology, raw material suppliers, and quality test methods can be crucial at many development points in which different routes to design and manufacture are still open. Decisions taken at these early stages can drastically alter costs and difficulties of quality manufacture during the NPI. This approach is part of the philosophy of *concurrent engineering*. Members of Marketing and Finance are also added to the project at an early stage to regularly attend ongoing project meetings, and contribute their analysis at milestone review meetings that are attended by senior management.

Such a methodology assures debate on critical issues relating to product features, manufacturing technology and costs, and avoids unpleasant surprises down the road. In a mature organization, every *NPI* step involves tens and sometimes hundreds of preparation meetings, systems tables, dashboards and charts. Every aspect of the products characteristics and readiness is continuously checked, marked and corrected by joint development and operations teams.

This mission needs to be taken in right proportion and with a lot of caution. As at early development phase, the product characteristics can be far from the product final configurations and operations work might not be effective. A rule of thumb will be that the seed team needs to evaluate their time investment at the development phase and its distance from product final configuration. Also a monthly cost calculating tool can reflect the above level of investment in order to prevent surprises in quarterly financial reports. This cost calculating tools needs to estimate operations support impact in percentage of overall **gross margin** results versus quarterly budget.

Another major advantage of the concurrent engineering approach is that the seed operations team which has accompanied the project from its early stages now becomes the owner of the Ramp implementation stage. This group has the maximum familiarity with the product, the technology and its problems in managing quality. Its members are prepared for the roles they must play, and are able to explain these issues to the other members of operations who will eventually take over the product responsibility.

It is important that all technology transfer methodologies will have a detailed book and process for transfer steps and stages of the new technology and product from research and development teams to the operations. The technology transfer document covers timing, activities, processes and systems for quality technology transfer from development to production. It starts from product early design stage (Design Objective) through its Laboratory phase to Alpha, Beta and pilot testing.

Figures 23.1 and 23.2 describes an example of the major *NPI* steps and flow and their document major subjects.

In mature organization, every *NPI* step has tens and some-time hundreds of preparation meetings, systems, tables' dashboards and charts. Every aspect of the product characteristics and readiness is continuously checked, marked and corrected by joint development and operations teams.

When *NPI* transfer system is well managed, with full transparency, coordination and in a *LEAN* way, product launch occurs with minimal financial deviations.

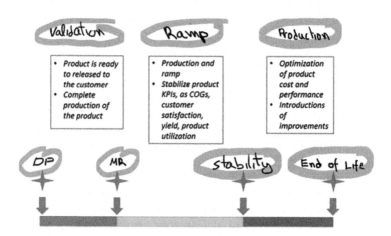

Fig. 23.2 Major NPI stages continue, their content and documentation

23.3 *NPI* Knowledge Continuity and Conservation

In dynamic organizations, *NPI* knowledge and processes must be constantly evaluated, reviewed and updated. The *best known methods (BKMs)* that were developed at product introduction must be revised in the light of new lessons learned. Furthermore, new team members and newly hired staff require training with the updated systems and documentation. If this is not carried out in a systematic fashion at the end of an NPI, important knowledge may disappear between one product generations to the next *New Product Introduction*.

Retain **NPI** knowledge and quality lessons and learns between **NPIs** generations, can win or lose the company next year P&L and market share.

One on One Meeting

24

One on Ones meetings, or as may be called differently, are important meetings for effective communication and driving excellence in operations. By now, we had describe several meetings while we reviewed major systems and processes for driving *operational excellence* in the organization. We had reviewed the importance of *LEAN* and effective meetings. *Assurance of supply* weekly meetings, cost reduction meetings, technical and *NPI* meetings. We will elaborate in the coming chapters on the importance of *safety*, *quality* and *yield* meetings (Chaps. 27, 29 and 36). The above mentioned meetings has technical characteristics, and serves the professional teams' forums and working groups discussions. However not necessarily they creates personal commitment of the participants. In order to drive change and improvement in operations organizations performances. Everyone in the operations, needs personally to be commit. Also reaching *operational excellence*, needs to be part of everyone personal aspiration. *One on one* meetings are the tool in order to reach personal accountability, between managers and employee and between peers in the operations.

> Trust, engagement, and commitment for personal and operational excellence achieves through one on one meetings.

24.1 How Do Trust Commitment and Accountability Are Built in Our One on One Meetings?

During our one on one meetings we give and get our weekly tasks updates, monthly priorities, quarterly objectives as our *annual feedback*. Also our personal and team objectives, and development discussions, takes place in our one on one meetings. These conversations links and connects between our personal results and the overall operations results. The connection between ours and the overall operations results

© Springer International Publishing Switzerland 2016
G. Issar, L.R. Navon, *Operational Excellence*, Management for Professionals,
DOI 10.1007/978-3-319-20699-8_24

versus the goals establishes our accountability. Also, our career path discussions, future aspirations, leverage of strength, and working on areas for development are discussed in our one on one meetings and connected to the above mentioned results.

Especially we care for the connection of our *personal development plan* implementation and future opportunities for development with and within the whole operations. As these discussions are relevant personally and significant for us. It raises our level of empathy and care. Both one on one meetings participants are interested, engaged and accountable for the meeting decisions. In our *one on one meetings* we continuously receives 360 degrees feedback from our managers, peers and subordinates. Sometime the feedback are less precise. However, feedback will always be more specific and effective in one on one meeting than in group meetings. This also raises our interest in the meeting.

24.2 Promoting Operational Excellence Accountability Outside the Organization

Once we had succeed in establishing openness, and commitment for operational excellence inside the organization. We need getting our counter parts outside the organization by in. As a first step, we need to persuade our counterparts, to step out of their responsibility comfort zone, and raise their *accountability* for the overall operations results. Without getting outside the organization counterparts commitment for improving operational goals, we might not succeed. Promoting departments and function stack holders commitment, as **HR**, finance, R&D, in our one on one meetings, is important for by-in and the success of the planned changes. In corporate work environment, we have business and professional interactions with other divisions, with other regions, supplier and also the company customer. In all those interactions we need to raise the operations performance bar and set high goals. With our counterparts personal accountability in improving operations performances we can drive a change.

> In our One on One meetings we discuss our work objectives, careers planning, and performance results, professional and business interactions.
>
> These personal discussions establishes our interest, engagement and personal accountability.
>
> Only solid base of personal accountability inside and outside the operations can drive change and reach excellence goals.

24.3 Preparations of Our One on One Meeting

Our *one on ones* meetings are not only routine and friendly discussion to sustain good communication and working relations. Although friendly discussions are very important to keep healthy cooperative atmosphere with peers and counterparts. Professional *one on one's* other than being with friendly atmosphere, needs to define the discussions objectives, to prioritize them, keep focus on their results, and time line for execution. It is important to define our one on one meetings purpose, expected outcome and future follow up.

For example, while preparing for engineering, technical or technology subject discussion, we need detail learn of the technical data, as **yield** or machine performance, software or chemistry process. We should define before the meeting possible solutions, and recommended path forward. Before budget, or financial decisions *one on ones*, we need to learn all implications of decisions on **COGs**, **Gross Margin** and **MOH** quarterly results. If we discuss supply chain subject we need to prepare supplier background, assurance of supply results, cost and quality performance. Data needs to be minimal and relevant, not in an overwhelming quantity. We need the subjects to be prepared in a well explanatory way prior to meeting.

For informative *one on one meeting*, we need understanding our business partner situation and prepare ourselves to support him with innovative out of the box solution.

Innovative and out of the box solutions are usually what expected from good partner when people asks for assistance in their one on ones meetings. If we had previous limited success with our counterpart. In the way he or she interpreted our message, and if we do not see any advance in communication after several *one on one* meetings. We can try and define ours and our counterpart communication dynamics and work for improving the communication gaps between us. In order to understand different communication dynamics, we can learn methodologies as *Human Dynamics* or other communication improvements techniques.

Keeping records of topics along the year, reflects subjects that advanced and subjects which were raised and discussed several times without tangible results.

24.4 Important Observation on Our One on One Environment

In companies with restricted space we may find ourselves locked in small size room, or using huge lecture room for two people discussion. Both situations are not creating effective atmosphere and does not encourage positive dynamic, openness and joint commitment. Such space does not flourish our openness and trust. In order to gain openness and good communication we need an environment that release tension. It helps to find location which inspires creativity and openness in one on one meetings. This alternative location can be the office building Garden, Cafeteria or Coffee shop in the neighborhood. Al those can serve as better locations for productive *one on one meeting*.

Very good preparation, existing understanding without friendly location, trough intention and calm atmosphere can yield shallow results.

> Inspiring creative and breakthrough results of one on one meeting requires trust openness and friendly environment.

24.5   Listening in One on One Meetings

It is our human nature to seek a leader—someone who will provide a sense of security, consult and provide the necessary resources for personal growth and improved performance.

Effective leadership is characterized by a manager's ability to identify his/her followers' needs and lead accordingly. Listening skills are the basis for this competency. Listening is not merely a passive action aimed at receiving a signal and responding rather, it is the deeper attentiveness to ones counterparts message and motivations, Boyatzis and McKee (2005), Segal and Horne (1997).

24.6   What is Active Listening and Why Is It so Important?

Stephen Covey (1996) discusses empathetic listening and stresses the importance of the listener's inclination to understand the counterpart.

Empathetic listening requires stepping into the others frame of reference. Once there, one can see the world as the other does, understand his/hers paradigm and how he or she feels. *Empathetic listening* requires much more than just receiving, mirroring or even understanding. Communication experts maintain that only 10 % of a message conveyed originates in the actual words we say. 30 % is conveyed in sound (rhythm, tone) and 60 % originates in body language.

Empathetic listening includes listening with ears, eyes and heart; listening to feelings, meaning and behavior.

When listening empathetically both the left and right hemispheres are activated; our intuition is activated, we feel!

One of the major insights, research on motivation provides, is that while fulfillment of needs is not a source of motivation, unsatisfied needs are. Psychological welfare and survival—the need to be understood, reassured, respected—are only second to physical survival.

When we listen to someone empathetically we create psychological space. Once the psychological space is created, we can focus on influencing or solving problems. Just as a doctor diagnoses before making a decision, we as managers, or peers must seek to primarily understand and diagnose before devising a suitable solution.

The field of Coaching also recognizes listening as a means for enhancing mutual learning and understanding between the coach and the trainee. The coach listens and is attentive to the formulation of the trainee's vision, values and purpose.

He/She is attentive to resistance, fear and symptoms of the trainee retracing his/her steps.

The coach tries to identify the trainee's authentic self and helps the trainee voice it clearly. *Actively listening* to situations in which "internal demons" challenge change, stress weakness and past failure, the coach assists the trainee in coping and overcoming these fears. The coach listens attentively in order to identify the developmental stage the trainee is at and assist in the journey towards self-realization.

Supporting an employee's personal development process is similar to the coaching process.

The first step towards understanding employees and their development needs, is listening. In order to better understand the (Whitworth, Kimsey-House, & Sandahl, 2006):

1. The 1st level of listening is internal. We hear the words of the other but focus on the meaning they elicit in us.
2. The 2nd level is focused listening. Our attention is focused on the other and the words they say (external focus, superficial listening).
3. The 3rd level is all encompassing. This listening is focused on emotions, body language and the environment (external focus, deep listening).

The coach, and in our case the operation manager, should use the 2nd and 3rd levels of listening.

The 1st and 2nd levels of listening focus solely on words.

The 3rd level of listening is based on all senses and communication channels; the manager is sensitive to the trainee's mood, rhythm and energy.

Effective coaching includes listening beyond the words of the story. The 2nd and 3rd listening levels enable the manager to access his/her intuition—the place where perception and sensory data merge.

References

Boyatzis, E. R., & McKee, A. (2005). *Resonant leadership: Renewing yourself and connecting with others through mindfulness, hope, and compassion.* Boston, MA: HBS press.

Covey, S. (1996). *The seven habits of highly effective people.* Tel Aviv: Oram.

Segal, S., & Horne, H. (1997). *Human dynamics: A new framework for understanding people and realizing the potential in our organizations.* Mississauga: Pegasus.

Whitworth, L., Kimsey-House, H., & Sandahl, P. (2006). *Co-active coaching.* Mountain View, CA: Davies-Black Publishing.

Personal Development

25

25.1 Personal Development Goals and Process

Often, the personal development process becomes ineffective because we tend to jump to solutions or hurriedly look for development opportunities. As employees and managers, we do not invest enough time and effort identifying motivations. Personal motivations are the basis for identifying development opportunities and setting development goals. Listening encourages dialogue, an atmosphere of openness, sharing and encourages delving into the generally unspoken topic of motivations.

Personal development process goals are:

1. Promote employees' personal development, self-fulfillment, potential realization and personal growth
2. Increase personal and organizational effectiveness
3. Align employees' skills and competencies to business requirements
4. Create clarity regarding specific employee development needs

The development process is continuous and not a one-time event:

1. By promoting employee—manager dialogue, the Career and Mid-Year discussions encourage employees to be proactive and manage their personal development process
2. Employees are responsible for their personal development, including: identifying strengths and gaps, clearly defining aspirations, writing and implementing their personal development plans
3. Managers are responsible for creating a supporting environment, guiding employees, identifying opportunities, mentoring, providing feedback and supporting development priorities

© Springer International Publishing Switzerland 2016
G. Issar, L.R. Navon, *Operational Excellence*, Management for Professionals,
DOI 10.1007/978-3-319-20699-8_25

4. Alignment between personal development and business requirements and challenges must be maintained

Our perception of work as a livelihood, a career or a mission influences our sense of satisfaction both from work and other fields. A manager who assists his employees to define and execute activities which the employee finds satisfying, meaningful and which can be performed well—will engage employees, create a higher degree of commitment and achieve better results. Three questions, once answered, may assist an employee in defining work as a mission rather than a livelihood:

1. What are my strengths?
2. What gives me pleasure/makes me happy?
3. What is meaningful to me? (Fig. 25.1)

25.2 Personal Development Conversation Model: SMOP Model

In order to help an employee focus on the process of self-discovery, which will in turn enable setting goals deriving satisfaction and pleasure; it is recommended that conversations are based on the following model and questions on the opportunities strengths and passion (Fig. 25.2).

25.3 Preparation for the Personal Development Discussion

In order to promote an empowering, deep and forth looking conversation, the following principles should be followed:

Fig. 25.1 The three areas for assisting employee defining his work as mission rather than livelihood

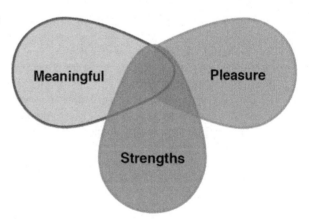

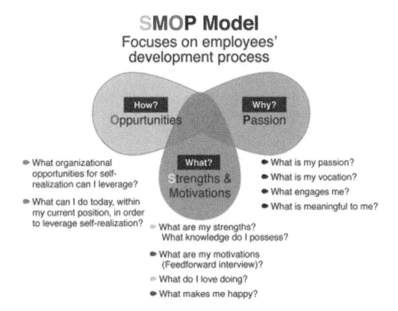

Fig. 25.2 Personal development conversation model—SMOP model

25.3.1 Creating the Right Atmosphere

- We need to show intent to listen.
- We need to lead and facilitate the conversation so that it focuses on the employee's strengths, motivations and passion. The purpose of the conversation is to define the stages for development in the organization.
- Focusing on areas for improvement may cause the conversation to stray; the personal development conversation should focus on positive elements.
- When the employee is silent, we need to listen. Silence can reveal a lot, it is our sense of discomfort that often elicits a need to say something, and break the silence. Silence enables the employee to process his/her thoughts and feelings, it may enable you to hear things you did not expect.
- We need to notice the non-verbal communication channels. 60 % of the messages we convey are non-verbal. It is therefore important we maintain eye-contact, and that our body language expresses interest in the conversation.
- We need to focus on the process and the conversation in order to identify the employee's motivations. We need not hasten to define development goals. The clearer the employees motivations are, the easier it will be for us to set goals and identify development opportunities within the organization
- We need to ask powerful questions—open questions which enable the employee to contemplate about him/herself. These questions empower and enable deeper cognitive and emotional processing

25.3.2 What We Should Not Do

- Not design the plan by ourselves before the meeting. The goal of the conversation is to engage and motivate the employee; a ready-made plan will have the opposite effect.
- Not dominate the conversation, the more we listen, the more we will learn about the employees and their motivations.

25.3.3 Discussion Topics and Structure

- Present the goals of the conversation
- Dialogue regarding the personal development model = SMOP and setting development goals
- Identify employees' motivations and strengths
- Career goals and aspirations, including current role opportunities and next roles to pursue
- Current role development for self-realization and to better position the employee for potential lateral or horizontal moves
- Summarize the meeting and discuss next steps, including creating or updating a career plan and scheduling time to continue the discussion

25.4   Literature Views of Motivation and Personal Development

Research and personal testimonials reveal a clear connection between setting goals and success. The correlation between satisfaction and setting goals is not as strong.

A goal achieved, does not ensure satisfaction. Goals are set so that we can enjoy the present.

In his article "Positive Affectivity" (Ben-Shahar, 2008) David Watson stresses the importance of the journey. He suggests that the attempt to fulfill goals, rather than their actual accomplishment, is the source of happiness and positive emotions.

The purpose of setting goals, which are future focused, is to increase pleasure in the present. This finding supports the existence of the personal development conversation in which goals are set, development plans are devised and managed—freeing the employee to enjoy and sense satisfaction from the journey.

In order to promote the process of setting goals for personal development, it is important to understand the term mission and its contribution to the process.

Psychologist Amy Wrzemesiewski and her colleagues (Ben-Shahar, 2008) suggest that employees view their work as a livelihood, a career or a mission.

When viewed as a livelihood, work is perceived as a necessity, the employee's focus is on financial reward rather than self-realization.

In this case the employee has few expectations aside of receiving his monthly income.

In contrast, an employee who sees his work as a career is motivated by external factors such as money, promotion, power and prestige.

This second type employee looks forward to being promoted, to climbing the corporate ladder.

An employee who sees work as a mission perceives work as a goal. Compensation and promotion are important, but work is amongst the top priorities because he/she wants to work. Motivation is internal, and there is a strong sense of self-realization.

Excitement and satisfaction are experienced while performing the job. These employees perceive their work as a privilege rather than a duty.

Research, conducted during the last decade, indicates that the distribution of these relationships to work exists across professions.

Reference

Ben-Shahar, T. (2008). *Happier*. Tel-Aviv: Matar Publishing House.

People Motivation, Productivity and Satisfaction

26

People's motivation, contribution, and satisfaction are essential elements for reaching *operational excellence*. There is excellent literature and extended knowledge regarding ways to motivate people in their work places and regarding the correlation between people's motivation and the organization's productivity.

26.1 The Sources for People Development Knowledge and Support

It is likely, that operation's managers encountered some of this academic knowledge during their studies, by reading management books, like the ones described in the *Books* section (Lundin et al. (2000)), or through sessions held by the **HR** department or external consulting companies. The four sources; Academic studies, literature, **HR** departments and external consultants, and classes are valuable to the continuous improvement and development of the operation's people's motivation, contribution and consequently to their satisfaction.

Many times these four major sources are sufficient in order to drive the operational organization to very good results and to keep the operation's team feeling satisfied, with their self-development, and feeling that their contribution is significant and well appreciated.

> Ask yourself if operations continuously measures its team member's level of involvement and contribution?

In order to monitor and verify that the operation's team satisfaction, motivation and contribution levels are high, an anonymous survey can be held. Its results will reveal the status of the operation's team and whether their level can be improved in

© Springer International Publishing Switzerland 2016
G. Issar, L.R. Navon, *Operational Excellence*, Management for Professionals,
DOI 10.1007/978-3-319-20699-8_26

order to reach *operational excellence*. Listening and collecting voice of the employee discussed in depth in its specific chapter.

26.2 Applying People Development Means as Routine in Operations

Once the team's satisfaction has been revealed and it has been decided to maximize the motivation and contribution in the operation's team. It is recommended to integrate discussions and attention to people's satisfaction and motivation in to the work week agenda. Routine discussions, by increasing the team's attention and motivation for excellence, are the first step to promoting *operational excellence*.

In many organizations, employee performance management is held, once a year, in proximity to personal and team development sessions. Also, development classes are held either with external or internal instructors once or twice a year. Over all development, performance and career management takes up to 2 or 3 weeks of the overall existing 52 work weeks.

As those activities are not part of the operation's managers and operation's team day to day agenda.

People's motivation, satisfaction, development and contribution are not a routine discussion topic in operations for 90 % of our working time.

This is due to the fact that "soft" subjects are not a part of the morning, daily and weekly routine meetings unlike the rest of the operation's parameters such as output, assurance of supply, technology, maintenance and customers complaints. The subject of people's motivation and satisfaction are usually postponed to periods when the organization's work load is lower. Unfortunately, in a dynamic organization, the operational calm periods are rare.

> Does your team has monthly work plan for its member's self-development and personal contribution?

We should treat people's motivation and contribution to the organization like every other parameter that is measured in the operation's department. With same high expectations, seriousness and routine weekly or monthly attentions which we apply for meeting every other operations *KPIs*.

Since the daily and weekly improvement measure of all operational matters are structured in the way of process indicators, just like processes of supply and demand and product technology performances. And since all operation's subjects are well embedded and mathematically calculated in the operations KPIs. The people, the "soft subjects", can and need to be embedded as well, similarly to the way mechanics, chemistry or other engineering best practices are. In that way, instead of having "soft" human related operation processes coming in a pulses, once or twice a year, people's motivation and contribution will be continuously developed by the teams and the managers. People related subjects would be treated, monitored, measured and reviewed on a monthly, quarterly and annual basis as every other operation's objective would be. This routine will effect employee, teams and the whole of operations, and will improve overall contribution and motivation and satisfaction.

26.3   Skills and Professionalism for People Motivation and Contribution Discussions

Sensitivity is required when continuously dealing with people related subjects and often there is need for professionalism and experience in working with soft subjects, the team members need to be very good listeners. Caring for people and openness are also important skills, as well as having relevant experience.

When dealing with people's motivation and contribution, only for the sake of receiving indications, without true sensitivity can create the opposite result. Routine work, on people's motivation and productivity, and a culture of continuous discussion of those subjects will establish a richer and more diverse people's culture as part of the operations daily work routine.

The results of a rich and diverse people's culture would not only reflect in the people satisfaction, but will also increase their contribution to the organization through:

- Innovation in operation,
- Lean thinking,
- Quality improvements,
- Technology solutions and many other of the people's "soft" skills.

In organization where people development flourishes, operation's results will improve and the team will reach *operational excellence* beyond their usual good or routine performance.

26.4   Professional and Literature Views on People Motivation and Contribution

Proof of the influence of people management on the motivation, satisfaction and productivity of employees can be found in many researches held in the field of Motivational and leadership studies.

Each one of these fields has examined a wide range of behaviors and the effect of the different styles of leadership and motivation development programs the workers receive on these behaviors.

Just as our health require maintenance so do team of people, although this sounds very technical, often we need to begin by adopting technical techniques which after some time are internalized and eventually become an established habit.

It's easy for us to ignore the need to manage the human resource, but managers who are committed to this resource increasingly discover how much their conduct with the employees influences their productivity.

The manager availability, accessibility and openness are the three dimensions of Inclusive Leadership, described by Kahn (1990) (Fig. 26.1).

The extent to which the manager is accessible, open and attentive to his workers, the extent to which he includes the workers in the decision making process, how accessible he is perceived to be by his co-workers.

These are all examples as to what workers are looking for from their manager on a day to day basis, not only in extreme cases. The more successful a manager is in creating the perception, among his workers, that the three dimensions exist in him, the more successful he is creating higher motivation among his workers.

Often operative management requires "putting out fires" and we get wrapped up in the assignment and lose the ability to see our co-workers, although they are always there.

A manager who succeeds in generating situations in which he is accessible, available and open to his workers will be able to create a work environment which will positively influence the workers motivation, productivity and satisfaction.

Imagine yourselves as the workers—all you really want is for your manager to "see" you, hear your voice, be attentive to you and be there for you when you need him. The big change which sets into motion our ability, to develop the three dimensions Kahn (1990) spoke of, begins when we develop empathy for our workers and can imagine ourselves in their shoes and understand their needs.

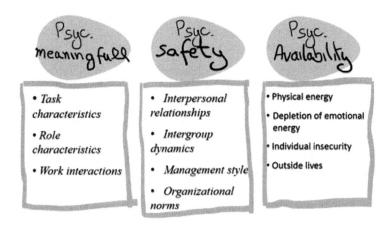

Fig. 26.1 Psychological conditions for work motivation (Kahn, 1990)

References

Kahn, W. A. (1990). Psychological conditions of personal engagement and disengagement at work. *Academy of Management Journal, 33*(4), 692–724.

Lundin, S. C., Paul, H., Christensen, J., & Strand, P. (2000). *Fish! tales: Real-life stories to help you transform your workplace and your life*. New York: Hyperion.

Quality

27.1 Quality Diverse Roots and the Way for Consolidation

Quality history in industrial organizations developed from the "*total quality management*" (*TQM*) philosophy in the eighty's to *quality management* in the nineties and up to *quality assurance* and *lean six sigma* methodologies nowadays. There are different perceptions to *Quality* in business operations according to the specific business's quality performance history and the business's evolution (Deming, 1994). Other variables in companies different *quality* philosophies are; product core discipline and product family and the industry branch the product belongs to. Different *quality* philosophies exists in pharmaceutical, semiconductor, chemistry and metal industries. The different philosophy's dictate the company quality processes, culture and consequent results.

When discussing operations quality philosophy, we need to remember that companies may adopt different *quality* philosophies and systems, or creates their unique *quality* culture and philosophy.

In many industrial business, operations are spread throughout different countries and regions. Product design, production and assembly can also be distribute in different countries worldwide. The combination of the four factors described: different locations, different quality culture and history, diverse supply chain and different industrial branch. All above conditions creates challenges for unite *quality* philosophy and practices in the operations throughout the product supply chain. In the described disperse and fragmental operation reality, common ground and common quality language are required.

> Uniform quality culture, process and systems in and between different business units along the supply chain enables high quality and *operational excellence*.

© Springer International Publishing Switzerland 2016   123
G. Issar, L.R. Navon, *Operational Excellence*, Management for Professionals,
DOI 10.1007/978-3-319-20699-8_27

Fig. 27.1 House of quality

House of Quality

Does operations has standardized quality processes, systems and culture aligned with suppliers and customers?

In order for operations performance to excel, four *quality* components are required: Quality processes, quality systems, quality culture and continuous improvement. All four need to be harmonious in order to hold together the operations quality house. Figure 27.1 schematically describes the building blocks of the operations house of quality.

We will review the critical components of the four pillars of operations *quality*.

27.2   Quality Systems and Processes

Quality systems and processes are the first to be implement in order to promote quality improvement in an organization. Sometime we underestimate the amount of different processes and systems that are needed in order to secure the product quality. A minimum of 20–30 major quality systems and processes are require to ensure quality. As quality performance is monitored daily, weekly monthly and quarterly. Our quality reports and the dashboards we rely on need daily to quarterly summations and accessibility.

For example yield reports, Human Errors, non-standards processes, quality audits and many other systems. All of these reports and systems, need to represent daily weekly and annually figures and trends. Falling to review systems and reports by the relevant time resolution can cause miss interpretation of the equality deviation.

For example: Large yield or no- standard deviation on weekly resolution might not be tracked on monthly report and vise-versa, a small change in yield trend can be followed on monthly chart and might not be tracked on weekly or daily charts.

There are several meetings to review quality results, solve issues and build plans for further improvement activities. All the above subjects as yield and process stability reports need the periodical forums and meetings to review them and improve results accordingly. On top of periodical monitoring and review systems and processes, there are product knowledge and documentation systems. Another important quality system is the quality learning processes from quality failures events, such as lesson learnings, and error prevention activities. Many of those systems are listed at the quality self-assessment appendix.

27.2.1 Quality Assurance Through Quality Dashboards and Workgroups

Product quality status needs to be reflected in dashboards, charts and key performance indicators (*KPIs*), along the flow of its life from creation through supplier and production. Dashboards, *KPIs* and charts are discussed in weekly and monthly meetings of the operations quality teams. The *KAIZEN* process, which drives product's quality *continuous improvement,* is an important system for promoting learnings from non-quality events. This will reduce the occurrence of non-quality events. Gradual improvements, after non quality events, will happen by practicing *lesson and learning* or *close loop corrective actions (CLCA)* processes.

> In order to secure our product quality, we need to implement extensive quality systems and process. We need to review the product quality continuously from many angles and resolutions.
>
> Quality reports, their routine reviews and improvement working groups are the base of our quality systems (William & Mathers, 1997).

27.3   Quality at the Product Development Phase

All these systems and processes take place once the product is produced and distributed to the customers. However before production starts, the initiation of product quality in the operation is rooted in the product's design in the development department. Quality systems start with the quality of process in product creation at the design phase. This stage happens inside R&D within the product's drawing software.

Quality design includes precise documentation and description of product specifications, its design margins, control limits and design for the product reliability. Once the product flows into the engineering and production floors, all data needs to be stored, checked and documented at the product configuration control.

Engineering and supply chain need to start quality programs from suppliers tier two, of subassemblies or raw materials, up to incoming quality check at the company or the subcontractor receiving material entrance of production sites. The described system has weekly reports of product quality from design through suppliers until the end of production. Any deviation needs testing, documentation and meetings to approve or disapprove of the quality status and deviations from the documented specifications.

In the product's early introduction phase (**NPI**), which has many stockholders, R&D, suppliers and engineering, robust change control systems and configuration control process are critical to ensure product quality.

27.3.1 Documentation

Along product's transfer process, from design to production and to the customer, technical data and knowledge need to be well defined, documented and trained. Any deviation from specifications needs to be reviewed and evaluated by the product quality experts from supply chain, manufacturing and engineering. In case of product parameters or measurements deviating out of specification (OOS) or out of control (OOC), experts need to troubleshoot the deviations with corrective actions.

27.4   Customer Feedback and Customer Complaints System and Process

There are several methodologies that can help the organization close non quality deviations quickly and permanently. The most important system would be getting the customer feedback once the product is in the customer's ownership and immediately implementing corrections. These corrections will improve the product's performance according to the customer's needs and satisfaction. The system for immediate customer feedback and effective correction process is very important for continuous quality improvement.

For long term quality performance, quality systems and processes need to rely on solid base of quality culture.

27.5   Quality Culture

The quality culture and philosophy of an organization are the organization long term strategic goal.

Only after practicing quality processes and systems for several years and after reaching a good level of quality results, can the operation adjust and phrase its specific quality philosophy and culture statements.

Fig. 27.2 Quality culture
fundamentals

Along the years, the company's management will learn their exact customer needs, their competition's quality level and the overall market trends in relevance to their product cost structure and its affordability (Fig. 27.2).

Quality culture fundamentals are: quality assurance philosophy and the quality processes and systems we have reviewed till now. Furthermore, operations need to have quality parameters embedded in its people management practices as rating and in people personal development plans, for example, increasing yield from 90 to 95 %. Lean six sigma practices, such as green belt and black belt, are a very important as part of the quality culture, both for continuous improvement and as a people personal development opportunity. Also in order to sustain quality culture, continuous quality knowledge and enrichment, need to be part of operations schedule. Quality classes and training examples are: systematic problem solving, Close Loop Corrective Action (*CLCA*) and continuous knowledge enrichment in *yield* improvement, **FMEA**, *SPC* and other important classes. A major component of quality culture is the commitment of management and managers as role models for quality culture.

27.6 Quality Continuous Improvement and Quality Benchmark

It is always helpful, if feasible, to aspire for the highest quality standards existing in the company's industry.

Aviation industry quality standards, for example, can be the highest standards for a company to benchmark with. Also, there are excellent best practices and quality success stories from leading companies that can be imported and adopted. One only needs to take into account that both quality improvement strategies, using high standards and importing best known methods, will take a significant amount of time to implement.

The quality learning curve is long, it takes a long time to educate people to reach the quality level and proficiency of a certified pilot, or it will take time to proliferate imported quality cultures from teams who have developed quality methodologies along the years, innovated solutions through many complex situations and quality taskforces.

Operations needs to aspire for best in class quality results in order to reach *Operational Excellence*.

Quality culture need rigid infrastructure of systems, methodologies and process.

Quality culture is essential for sustain of quality processes, systems and continuous improvement in operations.

References

Deming, W. E. (1994). *The new economics for industry, government, education*. Cambridge, MA: MIT Press.

William, D., & Mathers, J. (1997). *Change-ABLE organization: Key management practices for speed*. Mill Valley, CA: ACT Publishing.

Return on Investment (ROI) Calculations and CAPEX Decisions

28

When considering an investment in the operation's projects, we are usually limited by a restricted budget. The most common tool used to assess and prioritize projects is calculation of their *ROI*.

When we are planning the organization's operations annual capital expense budget (also known as CAPEX), a built in cost reduction component is usually inserted into the budget. We also plan on savings resulting from the routine activities continuous improvements, such as production yield improvements and quality and waste reduction projects. Through this way of calculating, we measure the anticipated gain versus the required investment, which factors in the *ROI* calculations. When sorting next year's saving projects, during the annual budget preparations, we will usually choose few anchor projects which have the highest *ROI*. Those projects will require a large portion of the annual CAPEX budget, mentioned above. Decisions on CAPEX investments, which are made during the annual budget process, will drive the operation's savings and cost reduction. In addition to the high ROI projects, we would like to keep some portion of the budget flexible, for ongoing initiatives throughout the year.

> Is the budget's capital expense allocation being managed through objective financial and measurable ROI indicators?

It is important to manage all of the operation's investments through a monthly budget committee, in which the projects compete for the required budget, and are prioritized according to their *ROI*. In these meetings, every department gives an update on the advancement in its cost saving project. The savings are calculated and are added monthly to the operation's overall monthly summations of cost saving. The overall savings are compared to the department's original commitments, as

---

$ROI = (Gain - Cost)/Cost$

© Springer International Publishing Switzerland 2016
G. Issar, L.R. Navon, *Operational Excellence*, Management for Professionals,
DOI 10.1007/978-3-319-20699-8_28

planned in their budget's estimated forecast. Establishing cost reduction meetings in the organization is important in order to improve future ROI estimations. With time the deviations, in the results of the actual cost savings or ROI estimates given by the project initiators, will be less frequent. Furthermore, through routine budget meetings the team learns, due to their experience, how to filter some of the "sugar coating", ask the right questions and challenge the benefits saving estimations.

> Ask yourself, does everyone in the operation's management know the ROI of the major cost reduction projects?

In order to prevent reduction in *ROI* along the project's progress, ongoing tracking and updating of cost and gains estimates are required. The investment budget's professional management, sometimes requires changes in the funds allocated between the different projects.

Safety

29

29.1   Safety as a Value and as a Priority

Although *safety* is the highest value of operations' organizations, it is important that we start studying it in depth only after we have already reviewed several of the operations topics and goals. We can summaries and phrase those goals in the operations mission statement as following: "The operations team will always strive to meet *assurance of supply*, with the best *cost structure* and the highest quality and technology through highly *motivated* and contributing teams". This mission statement is generally valid for most of the operations' organizations. Meeting this serious mission, including the five sub objectives, is not an easy task. When the operations does reach high results in all five objectives, *AOS*, *Cost*, quality *People* and *Technology,* we can certainly consider it as a significant achievement. The importance of *safety* in operations can only be understood after experiencing the complexity and the effort required in order to achieve the above mission statement. From the safety perspective, if all five mentioned core objective, *AOS*, cost, quality, people and technology were met, but not in a safe way, a serious debate rises whether it is a worthwhile achievement, regardless to the quality or cost results.

> Achieving the operations objectives such as **AOS**, *Cost Efficiency*, *Employee engagement* and *Customer Satisfaction* must be in *safe* way.

In order to reach a safe environment we can apply the same rational as the one reviewed in Chap. 27. Actually, many consider the subject of *safety* as an important sub subject under the topic of *quality* and culture. *Safety* systems and their processes need to be built first, the *safety* culture evolves after the systems and processes have been implemented, while we are educating ourselves for proficiency and *safe* behavior.

© Springer International Publishing Switzerland 2016   131
G. Issar, L.R. Navon, *Operational Excellence*, Management for Professionals,
DOI 10.1007/978-3-319-20699-8_29

We will review some of the safety systems and processes, focusing on the critical items, and especially on some 'out of the box' opportunities for people's innovation and personal development in this area.

29.2   Safety Classes and Content

Routine operations safety classes are: *Safety* of hazardous chemical, electrical hazard *safety*, *safety* rules for fire prevention, *safe* ways of working in heights, noise hazards, Pre Task Planning (PTP), Personal Protective Equipment (PPE), Ergonomics and a few more.

Opportunity for people development: preparing and applying **safety** classes and instructions hold within them an opportunity for people's development. People who works in specific areas, such as with chemicals or with electricity, can instruct their peers after they have learned their subject in-depth. This is an excellent opportunity for individuals to develop inside the organization and to achieve important personal growth with a minimal investment.

29.3   Materials Safety Data Sheet

Every plant which works with chemical needs to have all of the chemicals' data sheets ready to use on the production floor. All employees need to read the Materials safety data sheet's (MSDS's) in depth and understand the chemical hazards in their work environment. Team discussions and awareness of hazards are essential, as is the knowledge of specific chemical *Personal Protective Equipment* and its uses and the required response in case of exposure to the chemical. Furthermore, *MSDS's* are an important part of people's training and the knowledge continuously needs to be refreshed.

Opportunity for people development: **MSDS** gives the employees an opportunity to excel and to develop themselves beyond their defined professional roles. Technicians and engineers can learn about certain chemical's characteristics up to an academic level. These learnings are an excellent opportunity for personal development plans as well as for *innovative* projects for specific hazard reduction.

29.4   Safety Work Group

In order for safety to be a routine in the plant and a part of its daily agenda, every plant should hold weekly employee *safety Work Group* meeting. During these meetings, the weekly safety indicators, the safety classes' curricula and completion rate and the results from the safety management's walking around are reviewed. Safety meetings should not be technical and dull, peoples' innovative ideas for safety improvements, should create an interest and a creative atmosphere in the meetings.

29.5 Safety Trustees

In order to lead a safe environment, a core of the employees should pay a lot of attention to safety, on top of their routine work. Safety Trustees are the team's role model members for safe behaviors, they continuously educate their peers with safety knowledge and new improvements. The *Safety Trustee* constantly drives safe behaviors as well as projects for the improvement of production floor equipment, processes and behaviors.

29.6 Safety Reports

The *Safety **KPI*** needs to be reviewed weekly, or every 2 weeks. The safety reports discuss and show all of the subject's statuses and performances. For example, the safety knowledge status, **SMBWA** performances and findings, advances in improvement projects and safety events, all of the topics are reflected to the operations team.

29.7 Safety Improvement Projects

Many of the above routines' findings and areas for improvement, such as the Safety trustee's activities, SMBWA findings and safety work group meetings, generate safety improvement projects. The safety improvement projects are a part of the operations continuous improvements in all of the major fields of the production and safety in particular. Improvement projects create an opportunity for engineers to take initiative and for their professional knowledge and innovations to be manifested and contribute to the operations safe environment.

29.8 Log Out Tag Out

Log out tag out (LOTO) devices are locks, with personal picture tags that are used in non-routine work, for disabling hazards such as electric energy, heat, chemicals or gases. The devices disable and lock the hazards while the technician or engineer works on the production machine, doing maintenance work or any other work that involves potential hazards. The LOTO devices protect the worker from powering up of the system he is working on, by someone who has not seen, or is not familiar with the work currently taking place. We tend to connect the *Log out Tag Out* only to electric hazards, which is actually where it is most commonly in use. However all kinds of energies, such as steam, heat and contained mechanical energy, need *LOTO* devices. Also hazardous chemicals and gases need to be locked while their systems or equipment are being worked on.

Opportunity for innovations: The combination of the LOTO safety device and the system or machine, generates an opportunity for innovation. Since many times the hazards and locking combination are specific to the plant, the production system or the machinery, the team can innovate by designing a specific LOTO apparatus for its specific case.

29.9   Emergency Respond Team

Emergency respond team (ERT) is an important group when the operations work environment is constantly interfacing with hazardous energies and hazardous gases and materials. While working with chemicals and gases, any spill, leak or alert requires an immediate and professional response. This level of response requires special knowledge and training.

The ERT members go through extended training and learn about the nature and characteristics of the different hazards and the response practices in cases of emergency. It is a deeper and more professional level of training than the classes described in the training paragraph above. On top of the theoretical material, practicing drills and emergency events are important for keeping the team at high level of proficiency.

29.10   Safety Management by Walking Around

Safety management by walking around (*SMBWA*) is the most effective system for promoting safe behaviors and a safety culture in the organization. It consists of all four components that were reviewed in Chap. 22:

Uniting activities
Improvement through small steps
Consistency in performing the *SMBWA*
Continuity of the actions along the years

SMBWA unites all of the safety activities into one audit as well as coaching people on safe work and being a role model for safe behaviors. During our SMBWA tour we can check the usage of LOTO devices, we can review safety reports or check PPE, people's knowledge of the MSDS, the safety trustee's knowledge and so on. We can start the management walking around in small steps. During the first tours we can practice with only a few participants and for a few minutes a day and later on we can increase the number of participants and the number of occasions. The management's walking around is important as it is constant and always happening. It also it aligns with *LEAN* philosophy of presence on the production floor. Along the SMBWA observations, coaching and identification of hazardous material gaps processes, behaviors and knowledge are identified. These gaps can be closed later, not in a crisis mode due to a safety event, but as a prevention step for the next safety event. During later on SMBWA occasions the closure and verification of previous findings and the related closure activities can be checked. By doing all of this, the SMBWA serves us in identifying gaps, promoting continuous improvement through correction activities and finally by verification of the closure.

29.11 Personal Protecting Equipment

Personal protective equipment (PPE) is defined according to the hazardous materials that is used in the production process. Gloves and masks to protect from smell or irritation are the minimal basic protective equipment, the protective equipment continues to more complex protection gear as eye goggles or special breathing apparatus. *An important note*: As industry sometimes advances and introduces new invented chemical compositions and materials, before science has tens of years to evaluate the long term effects of working with the new material it is recommended, in order to be on the safe side, to take precaution and check the professional literature recommendations if the industry's experience in the usage of the material is less than 10 or 15 years,

29.12 Evacuation Drills

Although unpredicted events such as earthquakes or electrical failures rarely happen, everyone that has been in the industry for a long enough time knows that they can happen in every operations site. An evacuation drill once a year is important in order to keep those very low occurrences events in the organization's consciousness and in order to practice where to go in an emergency situation.

29.13 Safe Ergonomic

As in the office, many routines around the production floor, can cause an overload on people's wrists, joints, back, knees and other body parts. Routine observations and study are important in order to prevent injuries that appear after long terms and become chronic. Simple improvement projects, use of ergonomic apparatus and routine exercises, can significantly prevent injuries.

Opportunity—As with the safety trustee, there are always employees who are wellness and ergonomics minded. The employees who prioritize wellness, will be happy to promote a culture of ergonomic and an injury free environment in the operations.

29.14 Office Safety

Although office safety is not considered an area of concern, which has serious implications on operations routine, we need to remember that most accidents in the workplace happen in the building's stairs. Accidents in the office area cause absence from work and loss of work days. Furthermore, the more people keep a safe attitude in the office area the more they will develop their attention to safety hazards in and outside of work, at home and with their family. Also engineers will pay more attention to safety elements in their designs and engineering tasks, if their office environment also prioritizes safe behaviors.

29.15 Product Safety Regulations

There are significant amounts of product safety regulations in different countries and sales regions. These expertise's are specific to the product's family and are continuously being updated with complicated follow up documents and procedures. Usually in small organization the product's specific regulations are not common knowledge unlike the general and generic safety topics that were described in the above list. If the organization is not big enough to have a dedicated expert for the regulation of its specific product, it is recommended to hire a consultant. Not knowing all of the details and not receiving frequent updates regarding safety regulations of the manufactured product, can cause injuries or financial risks which is better not to take even the slightest risk with.

Ask yourself how many of the 14 safety processes and systems reviewed exist? And, does your team practice them routinely with high professionalism?

29.16 How Can We Keep All of the Safety Systems and Processes Routine, Crisp and Vivid Without Degradation in Our Attention on the Time? (Fig. 29.1)

As with time, our attention and crispiness to safety subjects which rise due to the operations daily life and routine, we can use practical solutions which keep safety routines and systems fresh and vivid all the time. This can be achieved through weekly and monthly cycles which focus on different safety topics every time. For example: every week or 2 weeks, different topics, out of the 14 safety systems and processes that were described above, can be the ones that are in the operations' priority and area of focus. These weekly topics can be discussed in team meetings, they can be the subject of attention at the weekly *SMBWA* practices, and the subject for training of the operations team members along those weeks. Along the

Fig. 29.1 The safe element
or the safety belt protection
from erosion in attention by
the routine

following weeks other topics will be chosen as the ones that are in focus, as we keep changing the subjects all the time. By this way of subject rotation, we practice every subject in depth almost once in a quarter and keep its knowledge fresh in the people's minds. By having new and different subjects practiced every time, all subjects stay relevant and interesting for the people to work on and to update them with new and innovative practices and solutions.

> Routine always reduces operations' awareness and effectiveness in safety. Rolling and changing topics keeps attention high and promotes continuous improvements.

Once all of the safety systems are in place and the operations has the measures for continuous improvement in the safety routines, people's safe behaviors and knowledge in safety improves. Those are the right steps to advance and establish a safety culture. All the above safety practices develop people's awareness and their care for themselves, their peers and for a safe work environment. Through these steps people reach the stage of full ownership of their safety performance. The steps in the development of the organization's safety culture from a bird's eye view are described in Fig. 29.2.

Fig. 29.2 Steps in the
development of safety culture

Supply Chain and Win–Win Relationship with the Suppliers

30

30.1 Win–Win Commercial Relationships Principal with the Suppliers

In order to achieve a breakthrough in the commercial relations with our supplier, and improve the supply chain's overall financial results, we need to change our view of our suppliers. Usually the first years of the relationships with suppliers are characterized by ups and downs. A WIN–WIN relationship may develop at the beginning of the commercial relationship, without paying the quality and production stop events learning fee, or the improvement of the relationship can occur only after incidents of supply shortages and quality failures with their corresponded cost. A healthy supply chain depends on straight forward, true, commitment and understanding, between the producers.

It help to remember that all of us, customers and suppliers, are part of a long supply chain. The supply chain starts from the producers of raw materials and goes through several suppliers before reaching final and finished goods. From a long term point of view there are no advantages to a certain producer's specific location in any of the supply chain location's. If any one part of the supply chain has an advantage over another, it is usually temporary and will rapidly change as a result of the fluctuations in global economy. Because of that, our first conclusion and recommendation is:

Our professional and commercial relationship with our suppliers have to be with a "no superiority and no inferiority" attitude.

We should treat our suppliers with the same standards we use for our own operations department. Relationships need to have similar high expectations on one hand and fair compensation and respect on the other hand.

© Springer International Publishing Switzerland 2016   139
G. Issar, L.R. Navon, *Operational Excellence*, Management for Professionals,
DOI 10.1007/978-3-319-20699-8_30

30.2   What Data and Knowledge We Need for Effective Win–Win Commercial Relation?

The first level of a professional relationship relies on our understanding of the supplier's product, processes and knowledge. We need to know our supplier's production floor in the same level of detail as we know our own production floor. Such an acquaintance starts with knowing the supplier's suppliers, and analyzing the risks of *assurance of supply* and *quality* to his raw materials and production parts. We need to learn about our supplier's sensitive spots, in the same way we know our own weak points, those which can affect our assurance of supply.

The second step is reaching a good understanding of our supplier's production floor machinery, processes and his capacity limiters. We also we need to understand the supplier's operational structure, department's people and culture. We need basic information on the supplier's principal P&L sensitivities for the product's price change, his potential for business growth and his motivation for growth. All of the above know how's support *LEAN* and efficient discussions and avoiding wasting management discussions on basic operations principles. We can be confident that the basic operations rules do not change between the sides of the meeting tables, whether it is the buyer's or the vendor's side.

We need to remember that having the above knowledge certainly does not change the responsibilities between the supplier and the customer. Knowing the supplier's operation in detail, still restricts us to different companies and different business entities. We should not take the responsibility of managing the supplier's assurance of supply, even if we are larger or a more experienced supply chain organization than him.

> Detailed knowledge of supplier and customer is needed in order to better cooperation, reach *LEAN* system integration and to eliminate waste and duplications.
>
> Transparent quality systems reduce material and *quality* checks.
>
> Unite *quality* goals, *KPIs*, measurements prevent waist, but keep ownership in each part of the supply chain.

Once the operations and the supply chain team have crossed the delicate ownership line, they will become accountable regarding the supplier's *quality, AOS* or reliability.

Win–Win business relationships with suppliers are based on:

> No superiority or inferiority
>
> Full *KPIs* transparency and mutual work on quality, cost and *NPI,*
>
> Continuous communication through meetings and join working groups
>
> Full accountability and ownership on product's performance from raw material, through productions to end product.

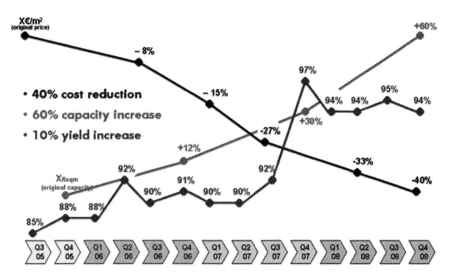

Fig. 30.1 Results of Win–Win relationship with supplier in the product cost, yield and production capacity improvements

Once these four practices are clear, all of the operation's teams and departments will have the same expectation from themselves as they do of the supplier's team, improvement in results will achieved.

Figure 30.1 (Ravoy & Faraggi, 2010), shows the results of 40 % reduction in the product cost, 10 % in the product yield improvement and 60 % increase in the production capacity due to Win–Win long term relationship with a supplier.

30.3   Systems and Processes for Maintaining Effective Win–Win Relationships with Suppliers

In order to sustain a healthy technical and business relationship, a net of communications with the supplier is built, and indicators for follow up on mutual goals are shared. If the supplied item is a critical part, daily communications with the supplier are established and hold the same level of importance as the internal communications practiced within the company regarding critical items. It helps to keep in mind that sensitive assembly parts or process ingredient do not change their level of criticality or sensitivity before the manufacturing's receiving gate. If a part or a material are critical for operations on our manufacturing floor it is the same level of importance that existed 2 and 3 weeks ago while the parts were on the supplier production floor. Because of that, the same level of attention and monitoring, through morning meetings, needs to be applied before our production floor's receiving dock. By keeping this rule in mind, we will not be surprised by missing parts for assembly or missing ingredients for production during the production process.

Product sensitivity and criticality does not change throughout the supply chain. Because of that same level of attention need to be applied before our production floor's receiving dock.

Routine reviews of the *inventory* levels the product quality and costs, as well as continuous improvement along with the suppliers, prevent surprises. Joint team knowledge reviews, strengthen the relationships and the COMMUNICATIONS and are not dependent on a single person or contact. Setting all the routines, structures and systems that were described establishes *LEAN* product operations. Looking from the product's point of view is important. It does not make a difference from a quality and functionality point of view whether it is a chemical, electric, software or mechanical part or whether it is a certain week at company A or company B. In any case the material flows between company A to company B and to company C. As this is the supply chain sequence, we need to focus more on the product's performance and quality along the chain and less on the business's artificial segmentations. From this point of view, the more holistic and continuous the operation applied along the product's or component's life cycle, the higher the chances for excellence in its performances.

Reference

Ravoy, D., & Faraggi, E. (2010). Building a solid interface with strategic suppliers. *16th Industrial Engineering & Management Conference* (pp. 1–5). Tel-Aviv: hp Indigo division.

Services and Customer Assurance

31

31.1 Value Product Service

This chapter describes the experiences and relationships between a specific range of products and customers.

We share the experience with end customers not wholesalers or distributors. Also, the product we refer to, has high value and its core is composed with high technology. Our assumption is, that this in depth and wide experience is relevant to a wider range of products and applicants. The basic assumption regarding the relations between a high value Product Company and the end customers is, that customers do not buy a high value product every other year. Much like most of us do not replace our car twice a year.

Buying high value machinery, technology or software products which demand a high capital investment, constitutes a significant financial investment which needs to be returned. Also their depreciation has a significant cost value in the upcoming year's customer P&L. Also the fact that the customer needs to purchase and pay now in order to secure future benefits and business growth is highly risky for the business. Because of the situation described, the customer's expectations are high in regard to product performance and supplier services. The customer expects his needs to be attended to, and professionalism from the technical team.

Technical Knowledge The product's technical knowledge and maximal product performance stand at the base of the relationship between high value product suppliers and the customers. The service department's mission is to provide the knowledge required in order to allow the customer to maximize the product's performance.

© Springer International Publishing Switzerland 2016   143
G. Issar, L.R. Navon, *Operational Excellence*, Management for Professionals,
DOI 10.1007/978-3-319-20699-8_31

> With high value Hi-tech products operating and technical knowledge such as installation, training, operating and maintenance are critical to the customer's assurance and we need to treat them as an organic part of the product.

Since knowledge is the core of competence in high technology products, the service department needs to develop product knowledge competence which is similar to that of an educational center. The competences are deployed from training and learning practices while the service team aspires to excel in the product knowhow.

> Ask yourself, is the product service department the company's knowledge center?

31.2   Technical Writings Team as a Base for the Service Department Knowledge

The source of product knowledge transfer and the start of the knowledge flow is, the research and development department. Where all of the product's technical details, drawings, functions, performances and work instructions need to be captured by the technical writers, and be well documented. However, as the development people are less experienced with the product's routine operation and its maintenance, the role of the service engineer and the engineering department is to review every bit of information and adapt it to the customer's operational environment, processes and procedures.

> All technical writing needs to be well accessible. Information needs to be easy to reach, friendly to use and self-explanatory. Accessibility and simplicity of knowledge usage in production environment is critical.

31.3   Training Materials and Classes

After having built the base by capturing and documenting the technical knowledge, the material needs to be translated into training material for diverse populations. Customer's operators, service people with different levels of expertise, engineers and manufacturing operators all need to have a common technical denominator.

The effectiveness and quality, of the training material and classes, final measurement is the product's performance at the customers' site.

If the product performs excellently (above 95 % utilization) it means that, the knowledge transfer did not decrease between leaving the source and reaching its final destination.

Once we have trained to our service engineers in the product's technical knowledge, any product failure on customer's production floor needs to be supported as soon as possible. On one hand, service engineers need significant technical experience with the product, and on the other hand they need, agile, structured and creative thinking. This combination assists them in solving problems with solid experienced databases as well as with updated learning and conclusions from new events arising. After the service engineer had completed his basic training, his next training objective is reaching proficiency and obtaining continuous updates and enrichment. In order to allow continuous learning and unified knowledge, a share center needs to collect all of the updates and feed them back to the service engineers in the field, after some editing and explanations. Routine meetings with the central operating team are required in order to share information.

The goal of service engineers is to create minimal product down time on the customer's production floor. This can only be achieved through a continuous flow of knowledge to the engineer.

In summary, the knowledge based continuous improvement concept contains several basic elements:

- Well documented, easy and friendly to use product technical knowledge
- Excellent training materials, classes, instructors, grades and exams
- Very well trained, proficient self-driven service engineers who are continuously learning.

Are all the three product knowledge components proliferated and practiced daily, and are they continuously improves by every service individual?

31.4   Customer Immediate Support Center

Once all three systems, described above, are in place, the service operations department can move to the next level of continuous customer support. This support can be any combination of on-line operation support. It can be active up to 7×24 or 5×10 or, any other intensive care service system that the customer needs.

The system, which answers the customer's needs immediately, serves as a control center or a control tower or any other centralized on-line response team. Such response teams have several objectives.

Such a system provides direct and immediate escalation from the customers and field service engineers to the core of the knowledge. Also the event is exposed to several departments as well as wider and different disciplines, knowledge sources and resource. This immediate escalation, although intense, is *LEAN* and saves time. These savings bring to cost advantage in comparison to the routine, three level system escalation.

The last benefit, of immediate escalation to a central response team center, is that not only does the assistance to the customer go *outward* to the field, when activating a response team the information is also flowing *inward,* back into the organization for improvement actions. All *quality* events, malfunctions or operations mistakes, are treated by the operations team within 12–24 h.

The immediate *Close Loop Corrective Action* (*CLCA*) is the most rapid, lean and effective system in improving product *quality* and reliability.

Using a service control center and an immediate response is most suitable in the *New Product Introduction* phase or, during stages when there are a relatively high number of improvements and action items. Through a rapid *CLCA* process the *supply chain* will immediately fix problems the supplier has, and the engineering and manufacturing teams will fix deviations on the production floor.

> The field Service control tower, though labor intensive, has cost savings applications as it enable immediate fixing of product deviations, in design, supply chain, manufacturing and engineering.

Team Work and its Development

32

32.1   What is Team Work and How Do We Test its Quality?

In order to answer the question it is important that we first define, what is a group?

A group is a collection of two or more people with reciprocal relations, who interact with ongoing relationship patterns, share joint goals and perceive themselves as belonging to the group. The "group power" is determined by the intensity of the connection and the interdependence between the group members (Rosenwasser & Nathan, 1997).

This definition mainly emphasizes the contacts between people and not the existence of a joint goal or common denominator. A common denominator gathers people into a category, but does not require a fabric of relationship.

Regarding the goal, indeed intensive relationships can develop out of complementary motives and out of different interests. Although, often groups form in order to achieve goals that can only be achieved by being a member of the group, such as a task force (Rosenwasser & Nathan, 1997).

But, when we refer to the managers' role as a team developer, at any of the stages of the team's formation and development, the manager must confirm and cause a situation in which all the team members know each other, understand the goals and agree with them, and maybe even form the group goals together.

Agreement and alignment with the goals is essential also in a situation in which the goals are set from above. Since even in situations like this the team has certain leeway to define the goals and translate them into their day to day actions. Defining the team goals, understanding the connection between the team's goals and the organization's goals and understanding the connection between every employee's personal goals and the organizational goals are a founding stone to the building of an effective team.

© Springer International Publishing Switzerland 2016
G. Issar, L.R. Navon, *Operational Excellence*, Management for Professionals,
DOI 10.1007/978-3-319-20699-8_32

32.2   What is Team Development?

A structured process led by the team manager, in order to develop and improve the team members' effectiveness, there for contributing to the achievement of the business results. It is highly recommended that this process takes place in cooperation with the employees on the team. The goal of this is to strengthen their feeling of influence and their ability to influence and to make them partners in action and recruited to the joint goal.

It is very important to structure the development process on an ongoing basis, since it promotes processes of learning from experience, research and improvement. The opportunity for team development advances a more open conversation about deeper emotional and interpersonal aspects than the usual work environment and there for encourages joint thinking, learning from experiences, shared decision making and later, implementation.

Team development processes also allow the team to learn about the other team member's skills and strengths. This can be quickly translated to the ongoing day to day work level. But in order to bring together the members of the team, in a way that is instructive and meaningful to the joint work, it is important to develop a positive atmosphere, openness, cooperation and open communication in the process. Ingredients that promote the attainment of effective development processes.

The process of team development is very similar to other development processes we know, such as stages of our psychological development as human beings. Knowing the stages of team development assists the manager in understanding the team's level of moral and the team's degree of effectiveness, and accordingly matches management tools required for the motivation of the team.

32.2.1 Stages of Team Development

Tuckman (Tuckman & Jensen, 1977) described a simple and clear model regarding predictable and known behaviors in every team stage. Tuckman's model refers to the team's development process which consists five stages- Forming, Storming, Norming, Performing, Reforming. It should be emphasized that:

1. Each stage builds on the previous one
2. Each prepares for the performing stage
3. Skipping any step effects performance negatively
4. With every new challenge process must be repeated

In the Forming stage the group members get to know each other and establish ground rules.

This stage is defined by lack of acquaintance between the members; the expectations from the team member's roles are unclear. Trust level is low. Team norms have not been established yet and there is a feeling that every team member is examining the other members of the group. A commitment to the group has not been formed yet.

This is why the team's atmosphere is characterized by insecurity and embarrassment. The members are busy defining external boundaries, there for this stage will be characterized by the search for common grounds. In light of that, the effectiveness of teamwork is low. This stage ends when the group members perceive themselves as a group (Tuckman & Jensen, 1977).

The basic task facing the group is to solve the issue of connections between the members and build the external boundaries around the group. At this stage there is a strong sense of consolidation around the similarities between the members and a sense of general harmony. At this stage conflicts are perceived as a threat since the group still doesn't have the internal strength to bear a conflict between the members. Therefore, buds of disagreement tend to be muted at this stage.

Following Tuckman's model, the second stage in the forming of a group is the Storming stage. This stage is characterized by the formation of roles and areas of responsibility for the group members and by not forming methods to solve problems.

The group tasks are a challenge; sub groups are formed; there are members of the group who create barriers; feelings of anxiety arise; competitiveness is created (there are group members who occupy positions of power and control); therefore, team spirit is low and the level of participation is not uniform (Tuckman & Jensen, 1977). Also when you examine the group leadership, if leadership has been formed, it inspires resistance (Tuckman & Jensen, 1977).

The Norming stage is the stage in which—the team is committed to a direction and goals, the team has the resources to execute the task, trust and appreciation are built, the goals are well defined, a constructive feedback is given frequently and received well, the trust level in the team is high, the leader and members of the team encourage the creation of positive norms, personal motivation is created.

The Performing stage is the stage in which- group motivation is high, the team performs efficiently, a feeling of satisfaction is formed as result of the group's success, there is a sense of group pride- openness, support, empathy and a high level of trust, the group maintains high functionality in spite of changes and new tasks.

32.3   In Order to Promote Effective Teamwork, Group Cohesiveness Must be Cultivated. Why?

Group cohesiveness is the strength of the relationships, that connect the member's one to another and to the group itself. On the personal level cohesiveness is derived from the inclination the group members have toward each other based on respect, affection and trust. On the group level, cohesiveness reflects the sense of togetherness that consolidates people into one unit.

Group cohesiveness is affected, among other things, by members of the specific group belonging to other groups as well. The group cohesiveness is manifested in the quality of the relationships between the members of the group and their willingness to leave it (Rosenwasser & Nathan, 1997).

According to Yalom and Leszcz (2005) the forces operating on all the group members are directing to stay in the group, or more simply, the pull the group has over its members. Members of a cohesive group feel warmth, comfort and a feeling of belonging, they ascribe importance to the group and feel they are appreciated, accepted and supported by the other members.

Pleasure and satisfaction appear more in cohesive groups. In this sort of group the members tend to share more and communicate more often. Absences from it are fewer. People in cohesive groups' sense increased self-esteem and reduced anxiety, probably because the group provides a source of security and protection. Cohesiveness contributes to the group's strength and vitality and increases the meaning of belonging to the group for its members. Groups' cohesiveness relates to their ability to answer their members' needs. Only a cohesive group can allow its individual members to satisfy their social needs. A group that is not cohesive enough can't supply those conditions and will not be a basis to satisfy the individual's needs (Rosenwasser & Nathan, 1997).

The group's cohesiveness creates an open atmosphere and mutual trust between the group members. This allows each member to be himself, to contribute and share their skills, opinions and ideas with the team. Therefore, in every stage of team development you, as a manager, must promote and encourage channels and mechanisms that will allow the formation of the kind of atmosphere described.

32.4 Examples for Question That Should be Asked During Stages of Team Development

- What Kind of Team do We Want to be?
- What are the team's goals? To what degree do we agree with the goals? To what degree is each one of us committed to the goals? What is holding us back from reaching the team goals? What promotes us to achieve the team goals?
- What norms/processes/methods exist within the team that we would like to stop?
- Which norms/processes/methods do not exist within the team but we would like to adopt?
- Which norms/processes/methods that exist within the team would we like to continue existing?
- Which norm/processes/methods don't exist within the team and we don't want to adopt?
- What are the team members' expectations from the team manager?
- What are the managers' expectations from the team members?
- What are the team challenges, and how are they being prepared for?
- What are the expectations from the team members with defined roles?

References

Rosenwasser, N., & Nathan, L. (1997). *Anthology for group training*. Zippori: Israel.

Tuckman, B. W., & Jensen, N. (1977). Stages of small group development revisited. *Group & Organizational Studies, 2*, 419–427.

Yalom, I. D., & Leszcz, M. (2005). *The theory and practice of group psychotherapy*. New York: Basic Books.

Theory of Constraint (TOC)

33

The *Theory of Constraint* (Goldratt, 1992) logic, that has controlled production lines from the 1990s, through the years, until now is the common denominator, in production line management, that was relevant 20 years ago and still dictates factory output. Although, over the last 30 years, advanced algorithms and automated mathematical tools, which improve line management, have been developed, they are all still based on the same principles, as those of the *Theory of Constraint (TOC)* (Goldratt, 1992). During the 1980s and 1990s in many industries, for instance the semiconductor industry, the production line was manually operated. But in the last 10 years production lines have become fully automated. Line management operated according to the *TOC* when the line was manually operated and it has remained that way, now that the line is fully automated.

TOC philosophy can be applied in many situations, not only to those reviewed in the inventory chapter; improving line management, line velocity and production line inventory.

Using *TOC* in all of the operation's departments can reveal bottlenecks and can continuously reduce their impact on production. In this way there is an overall increase in capacity in all of the operation's different departments.

There are a few basic principles to using the TOC in the operation's work environment.

33.1 Theory of Constraint (Goldratt, 1992) Principles

When managing the ***constraint*** in the operations, we must always apply the four basic principles of the *Theory of Constraint* (Goldratt, 1992):

1. Identify the constraint
2. Exploit the constraint
3. Prepare buffer before the constraint
4. Go to the next constraint in the production flow.

© Springer International Publishing Switzerland 2016
G. Issar, L.R. Navon, *Operational Excellence*, Management for Professionals,
DOI 10.1007/978-3-319-20699-8_33

In order to prevent production stops, constraint management is needed in all of the following segments of the operation:

33.2   Marginal Production Equipment Becoming Production Line Constraint

Production equipment is identified as a cause of line constraint if, it's inconsistent performance and unpredicted down time frequently stops the line. A rule of thumb for identifying the constraint is finding the place where work in process piles up before0 the production tool.

Once we have identified the constraint according to the TOC's first rule we *exploit the constraint* according to the *Theory of Constraint* (**TOC**) (Goldratt, 1992) by:

- Focusing on improving technical knowledge, in order to improve production tool stability, and reducing marginality through dedicated engineering resources and innovation.
- Cross training the knowledge held by the operators of the constrained equipment, in order to continuously operate the constraint, despite people taking breaks or being absent.
- Continuous engineering and managerial attention on improvement and troubleshooting, when production stops occur.
- Keeping enough inventory before the constraint, as a buffer for continuous feed of the constraint despite upstream of the constraint stop.
- Preparing enough spare parts to eliminate events of waiting for parts of the constraint.

33.3   Marginal Process Becoming Line Constraint

When a certain process step is marginal and the parameters occasionally go out of the control limits, the above TOC principles help exploit the constraint.

Continuous engineering focus and improvement projects are important in increasing the process stability and consistency. Deep investigation of the process's basic chemistry, electronics or mechanics, is required in order to increase its robustness. It usually help to reveal new process knobs which stabilize and prevent a specific process step from becoming a line constraint.

33.4   Knowledge Gap Can Become Operations Constraint

While introducing a new product, production and technical knowledge is still immature and has not yet been exposed to the operation's wide population. During this sensitive stage in the product's life cycle, the new product's technical knowledge may become the production constraint. Exploiting the constraint caused by the new product's knowledge gap is achieved by allocating all resources, training experts from the department, engineering and R&D in order to close this knowledge gap. Through intensive effort, learning the new knowledge documentation, instruction and training, the knowledge gap will cease to be a production line constraint.

33.5 Vendor and Material Availability in the Supply Chain Becomes the Production Constraint

In order to exploit the constraint we must identify the vendor's modules, processes or the part that are marginal. By using FMEA methodologies, holding weekly and monthly supply chain meetings with the vendor and preparing inventory as a buffer in case of supply shortages, we can prevent a specific vendor from turning into a production constraint.

33.6 Decision Support System Accuracy Becomes the Planning Constraint

As described in Chap. 4, if we do not verify and measure *critical* and *accurate* *KPIs*, or we do not review them routinely, somewhere in the supply chain, a part, a marginal tool, un-updated software or a server backup can stop the production line.

A practical lesson, which is always relevant to remember, when using the *TOC* principals is,

> The factor which is most active and vocal in drawing the organization attention, is not necessarily the organization's real constraint.

33.7 Managing NPI According to the TOC in Order to Shorten the Time to Market

As operations consist of many handshakes, constraint rise in every flow of material, knowledge or project in the operation. *NPI* is a chain of receiving and delivering prototype and improvement versions. Managing the NPI according to the *TOC* principles can accelerate the operation's critical product's time to market. Managing the *NPI* through the *TOC* principles means planning opportunities ahead of time and preventing line slowdowns due to constraints.

For example, when the *NPI's* first batch or product passes from research and development to the various teams in the operation such as, supply chain, engineering and production, if a module or a team is not ready with the new technology, part, design, knowledge or other new requisitions, any one of the above modules can slow or stop introduction of the new product. Also during the *NPI*'s sensitive stage, if a specific technical team does not provide solutions, by fixing errors, at same pace, the product introduction schedule will be delayed. If documentations or testing is not completed while moving the *NPI* to operations, the *NPI* process will slow down. The same applies in regards to training of operations for *NPI*, often at a ramp, new product trainers and knowledge availability become the product's introduction constraint.

Recommendation: in order to prevent first new product production stops due to the reasons that are described above, there are several processes that helps for increase production line to maximum readiness. One of the methodologies is "walk the product" which checks every single detail of the production flow prior of introduction of the product.

Managing according to the Theory of Constraint (Goldratt, 1992) principles and integrating activities such as equipment, process and NPI, prevents modules from turning on and becoming an operational constraint.

Reference

Goldratt, E. M. (1992). *The goal: A process of ongoing improvement.* Great Barrington, MA: North River Press.

Variability: Managing the Variability in Operations

34

Many industrial engineers and operations managers will agree that variability is the biggest enemy of an effective production system, as in every part of the operation exists its build in variability. We know that the production equipment is not available all the time, as well as parts for production, raw material and inventory are not always available. Our people and staffing as the production machines operators, technicians, and engineers whom we need in order to solve production issues, all of them are not just in time available when needed. From the product and process needs aspect, we sometime confront deficiencies of the precise process knowledge for running the production especially while introducing a new product, which is not always available when is needed on the production floor.

The goal of every manufacturing system is to achieve the following three objectives:

Maximize production line output,
Minimize product cycle time,
Minimize the production and product cost.

While the line output and capacity is largely dictated by the line constraint of every manufacturing system. Product cycle time, operating cost and product quality are defaulted by every step of the process.

It can be shown mathematically that were system has zero variability, it can nearly reach its theoretical cycle time. Additionally, its quality can be improved by a factor, only when production is consistent and well managed.

A prime example for variability reduction in every corner of the operations has been observed and reported from the Toyota production system.

There are several variability generators in the production as for example: the setup changes of the production machines, when we changes between shifts we introduce differences, when employee are having their breaks and there are always some differences in the level of the employee's proficiency.

© Springer International Publishing Switzerland 2016
G. Issar, L.R. Navon, *Operational Excellence*, Management for Professionals,
DOI 10.1007/978-3-319-20699-8_34

We have also machine un-planned down time that creates disturbance and change to the smooth operations and the activities of preventive maintenance which contributes to variability in the production line. Much more output, cost effectiveness and line velocity achieved when we control and reduce all the above variability contributors. There are several practices of identifying variability sources. We can model them mathematically, and then implement ways and practices in order to mitigate them.

Some examples for predicting and mitigating variability are:

In our production equipment management of performance, un-planned machine down time can be reduces and mitigate through preventive maintenance systems and technical discipline. Equipment management evolved significantly in the past 10 years in order to minimize unpredicted machine failures ant it is recommended to the operations members to study in depth especially the Total Productive Management methodology.

Another factor which introduces variability to our production line is operation people availability and the differences in their proficiency in the variety of the operations tasks. In order to reduce our technicians and operators variability in knowledge and proficiency, tight and continuous training systems, periodical enrichments and proficiency sessions reduces operative the variability of performances between the operators.

For controlling process variability effectively and reducing the variability both in production hardware and in chemical processes, we use Statistical Control System (SPC). SPC system is the most effective system to alert variability in routine production process performances. Charts and averages of production parameters along time are called the performance base line. Production base line can be any measured process over time that has statistical significance and has KPI importance. It is important to record the base line performance of the parameters, in order to identify any deviation immediately and change in production. Then, effective root cause analysis and quality measurements implementations reduces significantly variability of production processes root causes.

Although the path of variability reduction in operations takes long time and is full of challenges.

Innovative solutions and out of the box thinking are by far cost effective to improve and optimize operations.

Continuous reduction of variability can achieve through operational excellence process and systems as:

Systematic problem solving, close loop corrective action, preventive maintenance, training and proficiency, and all other process and system that were described.

All investments in the above variability reduction activities, are cost effective, *LEAN*, and cash flow savings to company bottom line. It has higher return on investment than investing in new plants building and buying more production equipment which has high variability.

Voice of the Employee

35

What is the 'Voice of the Employee'?

Voice of the employee is define as the discretionary provision of information intended to improve organizational functioning to someone inside an organization with the perceived authority to act, even though such information may challenge and upset the status quo of the organization and its power holders, is critical to organizational well-being yet insufficiently provided by employees, who see the risks of speaking up as outweighing the benefits (Detert & Burris, 2007). One of the significant components of hearing an employee's voice is creating a work environment in which he will feel secure- have psychological safety. But what is psychological safety?

Psychological safety is defined as feeling able to show and employ one's self without fear of negative consequences to self-image, status, or career (Kahn, 1990). It also refers to member's perceptions of an interpersonal context in which they "are comfortable being themselves" (Edmondson, 1999, p. 354). Four factors influence Psychological safety: interpersonal relationships, group and intergroup dynamics, management style and processes, and organizational norms (Kahn, 1990).

Kahn suggested that employees experience psychological safety, in part, as a result of supportive management and supportive and trusting interpersonal relationships with others in their organization. Individuals with trusting interpersonal relationships in supportive organizational environments are able to take risks, expose their real selves, and perhaps try to fail without fearing the consequences (Kahn, 1990 in Rich, Lepine, & Crawford, 2010). Research suggests that leader behaviors contribute to the feeling of psychological safety (Edmondson, 1996 in Carmeli, Reiter-Palmon, & Ziv, 2010; Nembhard & Edmondson, 2006). Specifically, Edmondson (2004) suggested that when leaders' exhibit openness, availability, and accessibility, they are likely to facilitate the development of psychological safety among employees at work. Nembhard and Edmondson (2006) found that when members felt that their leaders invited and appreciated their input, they developed a sense of psychological safety, in that their voice is appreciated and they are comfortable with speaking up and expressing themselves.

© Springer International Publishing Switzerland 2016
G. Issar, L.R. Navon, *Operational Excellence*, Management for Professionals,
DOI 10.1007/978-3-319-20699-8_35

Managers have a crucial effect over their employee's feeling of psychological safety, the more they succeed in creating an openness, availability and accessibility towards the employees the more the employees will share, raise issues, involve others and report problems, mistakes and mishaps, and initiate innovative ideas and solutions. Especially in an environment that encourages operational excellence, the more openness there is among the employees, so rises their ability to raise problems as mentioned in the chapter about Innovation in operation, there for encouraging an organizational culture of 'Voice of the Employee' will promote it.

Which is why, one of the questions any manager should ask himself is:

> How can we as managers, strengthen our employees feeling of psychological safety?

One of the effective mechanisms for encouraging openness is the organizational health survey that is designed to learn about: employee's perceptions regarding the organization and their managers; testing the organizations strengths; identifying problems and organizational rifts; testing administrative capabilities and more.

Hence, a survey is an organizational sensor which seeks to use the organization's employees of all levels in the purpose of collecting feedback regarding the organizational health. The matters included in the survey are diverse and are derived from the organizations values, organizational culture, the organization's business focuses, etc.

The survey includes issues relating to; direct management; organizational communication; rewards and benefits; teamwork; welfare; the organization's values; company management and more.

Since the organizational survey is a sensor, those leading it have an opportunity to define the issues around which there are an interest to check the organizational health. However, it is important that the survey have a basic structure that appears in the survey consistently, every year, i.e., a number of core issues that comply the survey in annually. Consistency in the issues makes it possible to identify trends and check improvement processes. Since the issues at hand test soft aspects such as: interpersonal relations; between and within groups and employee-manager relations, the existence of such a survey annually can reliably reflect trends and can constitute a measure for checking the effectiveness of intervention processes in these aspects.

An organizational survey held systematically every year sends the organization's employees the message that their voice is important and the company's management views them as partners in action and in the improvement of the organization.

But, that is not sufficient to establish the employees trust in the tool and to strengthen their willingness to share and make their voices heard, the company's management must deal with the feedback (even if it is not all pleasant) and to lead the improvement processes derived from the survey.

In order to make the improvements that are derived from the survey effective and allow them to be assimilated over time, it is important that the employees take a part in developing solutions for the areas that survey recognized as areas in need of improvement.

> The manager's role is to enhance among his employees the feeling that they can affect what goes on in the work environment, with their co-workers and in their relationship with him as their direct manager.

In the Sect. 38.3.4 of this chapter appears a comprehensive questionnaire which includes several question regarding diverse issues for the organizational health survey. It is important to emphasize that it is highly recommended that at the end of the quantitative section of the survey the employees be asked two open questions. One which seeks to find out, what are the points of strength that exist in the organization, and a second which seeks to identify two areas requiring improvement on the organizational level. The open section is a fertile ground for the employees to float ideas and direct the spotlights towards specific matters that occupy them and that they were not necessarily asked about in the quantitative survey.

In summary, as a manager leading processes that encourage hearing the voices of the employees you should:

- Recognize the issues on which you would like to receive annual feedback.
- Establish trust, openness, accessibility and psychological availability among your employees so they can make their voice be heard.
- Use the organizational health determination survey as a sensory tool in order to identify organizational strengths and areas in need of improvement.
- Encourage all employees to answer the survey. If as many employees as possible answer the survey the picture received will truthfully reflect the current situation in the field.
- After processing the survey's data communicate them back to the employees and give an update regarding the processes that will be derived from the survey.
- Cooperating with the employees in the thinking process and in leading change and improvement process is required in order to build an organizational culture that constantly promotes improvement.
- Remember that the survey can be held on a organizational level or on a limited level regarding defined groups.

References

Carmeli, A., Reiter-Palmon, R., & Ziv, I. (2010). Inclusive leadership and employee involvement in creative tasks in the workplace: The mediating role of psychological safety. *Creativity Research Journal, 22*(3), 250–260.

Detert, J. R., & Burris, E. R. (2007). Leadership behavior and employee voice: Is the door really open? *Academy of Management Journal, 50*(4), 869–884.

Edmondson, A. C. (1999). Psychological safety and learning behavior in work teams. *Administrative Science Quarterly, 44*(2), 350–383.

Edmondson, A. C. (2004). Psychological safety, trust, and learning in organizations: A group-level lens. In R. M. Kramer & K. S. Cook (Eds.), *Trust and distrust in organizations: Dilemmas and approaches* (pp. 239–272). New York: Russell Sage.

Kahn, W. A. (1990). Psychological conditions of personal engagement and disengagement at work. *Academy of Management Journal, 33*(4), 692–724.

Nembhard, I. M., & Edmondson, A. C. (2006). Making it safe: The effects of leader inclusiveness and professional status on psychological safety and improvement efforts in health care teams. *Journal of Organizational Behavior, 27*, 941–966.

Rich, B. L., Lepine, J. A., & Crawford, E. R. (2010). Job engagement: Antecedence and effects on job performance. *Academy of Management Journal, 53*(3), 617–635.

Yield, Improvement and Sustaining High Yield
36

36.1 Yield and P&L Bottom Line

Many times, in industrial organizations, there is no clear operational connection between the balance sheet numbers, financial results and material waste, which is distributed in many processes in the organization. People do not always realize the huge potential that yield improvement and waste reduction hold for the company's P&L. Also, people's contribution in innovations for yield improvement projects is not always leveraged to its maximum potential. An important factor in the prioritization of work in operations is that, an increase of the product's yield and a substantial reduction of waste and scrap are the most effective form of net saving in operations.

> Yield net savings flows through to the company's bottom line directly, and improve the company's **Gross Margin** and net profit by same cash amount.

Studying yield improvement practices of many case study from several disciplines. From operations of biology products, semiconductor industry, chemical and hardware industries. We can see that solving yield issues fundamentals and principle mechanisms are similar cross industries.

36.2 Product Yield Targets and Capacity

The first question a process and yield engineer is confronted with, while working on yield improvement, is what are the process's yield capabilities? When a process is released from research and development to operations, the first yield numbers can be very low, from 10 to 40 %. At that stage, the operations team is not sure whether they can make it and meet the high yield numbers 80–90 %. Although when starting

© Springer International Publishing Switzerland 2016
G. Issar, L.R. Navon, *Operational Excellence*, Management for Professionals,
DOI 10.1007/978-3-319-20699-8_36

from low yield numbers there is a long and steep path to climb, a low yield starting point does not necessarily predict the feasibility of reaching a yield of 95 % and above. Though it might take several years and a few engineers, reaching a yield of above 95 % &, is possible even when starting from a yield of 20 %.

> Ask yourself whether your yield improvement team can bring product's yield from 30 to 40 %, to a yield of 90 and 95 %?

Yield, analysis methodologies and relevant statistical tools are operations knowledge. This knowledge needs to retained and continuously developed between generations of products.

36.3   Steps and Timing of Yield Improvement

The first action the yield improvement team should perform in order to find the major contributors to yield loss, is the Pareto analysis. The Pareto charts, of the major yield offenders, need to be reviewed after every production run. If the yield offenders working hypothesize are correct in every run, day and week, the higher offenders' values need to trend down. Also, if the working hypothesize is correct, a standard deviation of the runs values in every production process, needs to be diminished as we advance with the process of controlling the root causes for the yield decrease.

Before automatically starting with the major contributors to the yield drop, we need to evaluate the time prediction for solutions and implementation, since the time we invest in yield improvement is a major financial factor, due to amount of scrap produced while studying the yield. Sometime it will be more cost effective to bucket several yield contributors and rapidly prevent money loss due to scrap, than to focus on one yield contributor with a longer solution time. The yield improvement time dynamic is demonstrated in the Fig. 36.1 chart.

As we can see in the chart yield improvement has three major phases:

In phase one, the contributors to the low yield are the major's ones. Solving these major offences will bring the product yield an increase in step function of tens of percent, within a relatively short time. In phase two, finding the root cause takes longer and the improvement rates are only a few yield points for every solution implemented successfully, this stage can also take several months. The third phase may take several quarters, this step is characterized by small increments, less than 1 % of yield at a time. Every improvement and solution that we successfully implement contributes less than 1 % to the yield gain. The last phase is sustaining the product's yield and preventing it from rebounding and dropping back to the low numbers. In this part of the product's life cycle, yield work may take until the end of the product's life. During this stage detailed and consistent work is required in order

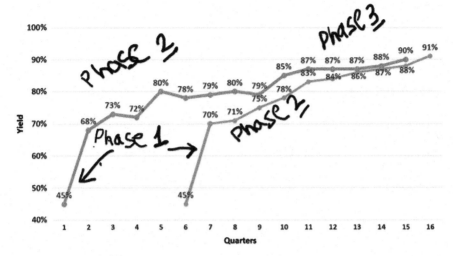

Fig. 36.1 Examples of 4 years of investment in products yield improvements and their results

to sustain high yields and prevent significant yield drops. We will elaborate on this challenge later.

Improvement of yield according to the 'higher yield offenders first' is also important from a costs and accounting perspective. When the product production ramp takes several months, due to low production volumes, the scrap level at the ramp's beginning are significantly lower than at full ramp when production quantities are high.

Therefore, solving major yield offences has a limited "grace time" due to low production volumes. During that stage, low production volumes create low levels of material scrap and consequently a minimal loss of money. This is a significant financial opportunity for future savings, when production volumes are high and the yield has stabilized, before the high production volumes.

> Yield improvement at an early stage is cost effective, as it is before the product ramps to high production volumes and cause a high financial burden due to scrap.

36.4   Sustaining High Yield Over Time

When a product's production descends, due to low demand, a risk of significant money loss arises again. This is due to, less focus on yield control and an increase in the instances of yield drops. This situation usually happens when an organization shifts its attention to the next, new product. At this stage most resources are, very reasonably, depleted and are allocated to the new product's first phase of yield improvements.

There are a few systems and processes that can secure the product's yield from dropping, during the sustain phase:

- Training manufacturing technicians in the engineering process and product yield knowledge.
- Empowering manufacturing technicians to control yields through statistical process control (SPC).
- Routine line management, with line stops that segment the line. Stopping the line and activating a task force when yield drops.
- Keeping low inventory between yield control steps, in order to reduce the risk in case of a yield drop.

Although product may be towards end of life. It is important to keep high attention and focus on high yields, as the long journey practices and experience to reach those numbers may quickly forgot.

Where, When and How We Can Apply the Operational Excellence Concise Guide Methods?

37

By now, going over the recommendations, the reader had the information on operational excellence practices. Probably he asks himself how when and where are the most favorite conditions in order to begin their implementation along the life of the operations and the company.

As the recommendations are not restricted to a certain industry, region or culture. It can implement in wider operations communities, in the Hi technology industry, as well as in the traditional and any other industry. There are no preferences were to start implementing the guide practices.

37.1 Where? and When We Can Start Implementing the Guide Recommendations?

There are several imposed situations on the business that we can trigger and leverage as an opportunity to use the recommendations and start their implementation. When a production line, or any other operations activity, moves to another region or sites, as from the US to Europe or to Asia, or between different countries in Europe or in Asia, in this cases we can use the guide as a common language for working together on joint goals, between the different sites or regions teams.

Another situation in company life is when our plant went through acquisitions by larger company, or if we work in a large company that had bought small vendor or competitor. In these cases we can use the guide recommendations in order to clarify and bridge systems and processes gaps between the different operations teams. We can map effectively differences in the way measurements and KPIs are practiced, differences in systems, processes and culture and build a joint plan can which rapidly can be set in order to resume the operations despite the change in company ownership.

We can use the self-assessment questionnaires to align on the level of the gaps between different companies or sites.

© Springer International Publishing Switzerland 2016
G. Issar, L.R. Navon, *Operational Excellence*, Management for Professionals,
DOI 10.1007/978-3-319-20699-8_37

Once the gaps are known, it is easier to have an effective discussion between the parties and set mutual goals with detailed plans for closing the gaps. Many times, each party will brings to the table strengths that the other team is missing. So gap closure can works in both directions and the over all of the equation can be higher than the starting point.

Another opportunity using the guide for operational excellence, is when operative teams are part of same supply chain but are from different companies or located in different regions or countries. Teams may encounters differences in the operations habits, philosophies and codes of communication of their vendor or supplier. Using the guide methodologies will bridge those gaps fast and will consolidate different parties to one joint and functioning team. Similar case happens with in the same company but between different departments. For example between R&D department, and sales and between the operations department. Or when different departments are distributed between different regions. While they needs a common references to communicate with same operational baseline, otherwise their product launch or production will not be manage successfully and might miss marketing schedule.

37.2 How Should We Implement the Guide Recommendations?

Our major recommendation for the implementation of our guide philosophy is through *small steps*.

As reaching operational excellence takes 2–3 years of journey. Starting with few specific topics will bring first notable changes after 3–4 months. For example we can start with improving *Safety*, *quality cost* or *NPI* through *small steps*. Saying small steps we mean, working with teams on implementing of one system at a time and staggering their implementation one after the other. Every week we can check the improvement in the weekly performances and gradual improvement of the system and the process we are focusing on. After recognizing improvement we can move to the next system and process.

37.3 Who Should Be the Team that Implement the Recommendations?

We recommend to use the manual for the entire operations community. This guide is relevant to manufacturing supervisors, engineers and to managers. Also services people, supply chain and planning people can benefit from applying the recommendations. We suggest the guide to all different levels in the organizations to the operation Directors and General Managers as well as to the first line managers and engineers. We recommend it to the different disciplines, to the industrial engineering community and student's researcher and students in order to enrich their learnings experiencing actual operations daily life views. The guide can help the Human Resource community, HR managers and individual contributors, it can enrich finance people as CFOs and controllers. One might debate how come the guide practices are relevant for supervisor, engineer, CFO and GM? As the guide is rooted in the practical reality of business operations, we share the business integrative view and improving performances that can serve different business stack holders. For example the finance expert will see other than his professional view and parameters as COGs and Gross Margin, the industrial engineer limiters and calculated factors, as DOI, the people management view as satisfaction results, and the technologist view and all will benefit from the integrated balance score card.

It is always enriches and refresh our perspective with a different operative angle. Especially while purpose is to advance the unite operations team to excellence and the company to better P&L results.

The concise guide can assist research and development people who needs to launch or ramp designed product with tight interfaces with the operations. In cases which research and development and operations departments are located in different countries, the guide establish a common language for communicating also without face to face meetings. Using the knowledge through audio conferences and through correspondence through e mails.

Appendices

38

38.1 Appendix A: Recommended Books for the Study and Practice of Operational Excellence

Business operation books are always nice as a present at the end of a team building event, or as a farewell present when one of the team members is moving to a new position in or outside the operation. We also give or receive operations guides at the end of training sessions or development classes.

Occasionally, while we are waiting for our connection flight on a business trip, we may find ourselves standing in front of the business books shelve at the bookstore on the way to our flight gate.

With Lean thinking on our minds, we have consolidated some of the most important studies of operational excellence into a concise list of a few books. Though we need to remember that business operations books, are written according to the writer's personal philosophy and experience, and we need to consider their implementation with caution, in small steps while carefully watching the results, as we have previously recommended.

First book we are recommending, for practice which always brings benefits, is the '*7 habits for highly effective people*' *by Steven Covey* (Covey, 1996). For over two decades *Covey's* philosophy and his book have been a thorough companion to operations professionals. The *7 habits*, serves as a compass, to help us define where to go to through the *start with end in mind* habit and how to advance through the habit of *being proactive*.

These two practices especially help the operations team to navigate through the turbulence of the business operation's waters. The CD version with *Covey's* magnetic voice is excellent for listening to while driving to and from work. *Covey's* philosophy and recommendations also help by reflecting on our daily business operations and comparing them with *Covey's* examples.

Another major take away from *Covey's* book is the knowledge regarding prioritization of our tasks and objectives by doing "*first things first*" which is a core skill for operations.

© Springer International Publishing Switzerland 2016
G. Issar, L.R. Navon, *Operational Excellence*, Management for Professionals,
DOI 10.1007/978-3-319-20699-8_38

Are 'being proactive' and putting 'first thing first' a common practice and culture of the operations team?

Once the operation's team members know *where* are they heading and *why*. The second important lesson is to identify the operation's *bottleneck* or the operation's *constraints,* which slow down the operation's advance. Bottlenecks delay the operation in successfully reaching the company's and the department's goals.

The *theory of constraint* by Eliyaho Golderath (Goldratt, 1992) is the philosophy which reveals the importance of identifying and solving the operation's bottlenecks. Golderath's book *'the Goal'* is accepted world-wide as an excellent explanatory guide to the *Theory of constraint.* The **Goal's** knowledge is always relevant on the production floor, in the supply chain, services and in all of the other operation's disciplines. Operations, by design, are always confronting resource and financial limitation. The **Goal** teaches the operations team how to deal with the constraint as a routine and as a part of their daily life, and not be as surprised as they would be if it was an unexpected or singular event. A thorough understanding of living with constraint, as an integral part of the operation, helps the production planning, control and others, to search daily for limiters and solutions.

After the operations team knows how to define the right operational goals and what bottlenecks they need to overcome in order to reach them and practices it, the third lesson is the teamwork way for reaching those goals. Operations team motivation and winning spirit, is the third important knowledge to read and learn about, as it is important that reaching the operation's goals will be done by all of the operations team members together. *'Gung Ho'* by Ken Blanchard and Sheldon Bowles, (Blanchard & Bowles, 1998). Tell the story of raising people's motivation and getting a business back to its core values. *'Gung Ho'* gives the principles and values for building team motivation and increasing their contribution, by simple lessons.

Another book about motivation, team spirit and enthusiasm is *'Fish'* (Lundin, Christensen, & Strand, 2000). The book and the movie have good real business life examples and techniques, that come from a fish shop in Seattle. The fourth operational educational step, after learning the *will to win* spirit and learning how to develop team motivation, is learning how to develop soft people skills.

There are several important methodologies which help maximize the effectiveness of developing soft people skills. One of the methods is identifying people's strength using the *'Gallop'* survey and the book *'Now Discover Your Strengths'* by Buckingham and Clifton (Buckingham & Clifton, 2001). The book is based on a large amount of statistical data regarding different people strengths, regardless to country or culture.

As *operational excellence* depends on coordination between departments, teams and individuals, identifying and building teams that have diversity and complementary strengths will serve as an order multiplicand. A dynamic operation, which includes moving people to different assignments is important. Learning to identify people's strength significantly helps in the optimal assignment of people. For broadening the knowledge on leadership which resonate to different employees dynamics and people strengths *Resonant Leadership* by Boyatzis and McKee is (Boyatzis & McKee, 2005) is an excellent guide.

Malcolm Gladwell and his book on Outliers (Gladwell, 2008) gives a time perspective to how long we need to practice and invest in order to reach *operational excellence*.

Other effective tactics and operations structures are well described in 'Change Able organization' by William Daniels (Daniels & Mathers, 1997).

There are three major steps to reaching operational excellence according to the above book:

Learning to be proactive, plan ahead and prioritize the operation's objectives and tasks by importance

Identifying the operation's constraints and the ways to overcome them

Developing individual and the team motivation and skills, in order to reach the operation's goals together.

Other than the three practices above, general business books are always inspiring and enriching, especially when we read about world icons leadership in the industry, such as Steven Jobs and the Apple turnaround story described in his biography. A relevant history fact which is not widely known is that Jobs implemented operational best practices, such as significantly reducing inventory and types of products, when he returned back to Apple (Isaacson, 2012).

There are excellent learnings in 'Iacocca Ford story (Iacocca & Novac, 1984), and the Gerstner IBM transformation (Louis & Gerstner, 2002) as well as in many other inspiring and exciting stories about industries rise from loss to profit.

The classic books and research on success in Collins 'Build to last' (Collins & Porras, 1994) and 'Good to Great' (Collins, 2001) are an excellent overview on companies' long term success.

As trends and common practices are different and change every several years, and since new managerial and operational philosophies rise from time to time, we can start with the books whose values have been recognized by many operation professionals over the years and the core philosophies that were adopted in different industries and markets, and who are less sensitive to trends.

As recommended in the *Gung Ho* story:

It is better to hold on to the rocks than on to the pebbles, especially in turbulent water.

Operations practices are continuously developed by a professional and experienced team. We need to enrich ourselves with updated operations knowledge, as commonly done in all other engineering and technology disciplines.

38.2   Appendix B: List of Content by the Different Operations Departments and their Disciplines

Manufacturing

Safety
Quality
Cost of Goods (COGs)
Out-put through Assurance of Supply (AOS)
People management: one on ones, Personal Development, Empowerment.
Manufacturing Excellence in Daily Life

Engineering

Failure Mode Effective Analysis (FMEA)
New Product Introduction (NPI)
Yield improvement
Engineering People development through Innovation
Cost Reduction described in the COGs chapter

Planning and Control

Supply and Demand through Assurance of Supply chapter (AOS)
Control through Decision Support Systems (DSS) chapter
Inventory control by Days of Inventory (DOI)
Just In Time (JIT)
Key Performance Indicators (KPIs)
Variability and its control in the operations

Financial Control

Cost of Goods (COGs)
Gross Margins (GM)
Manufacturing Over Head (MOH)
Return on Investment (ROI)

Supply Chain
  Services and Customer assurance

People Management

Empowerment
Human Resources
Leadership in Operations
One on Ones
Personal Development
People Motivation and Contribution
Voice of the Employee

General

Books on Operational Excellence
e mails management
Innovation in Operations
Interfaces in Operations
Lean
Effective Meetings
Theory of Constraint (TOC)

38.3   Appendix C: Self-Assessments

38.3.1 Quality Self- Assessment

			Do not exist Score = 1	Exist but rarely used Score = 2	Exists and routinely used Score = 3	Exists routinely used and continuously improves Score = 4	Remarks
1. Knowledge and training	1.1	**Are the product and process are well documented and described**					
	1.2	Are there basic operation training packages Level 1?					
	1.3	Are there advanced training packages Level 2 and L3?					
	1.4	Are there certification process for the different packages?					
	1.5	Is engineering and training expert holds the training and certification?					
	1.6	Are record kept and updated of the certification level of each employee?					

(continued)

			Do not exist Score = 1	Exist but rarely used Score = 2	Exists and routinely used Score = 3	Exists routinely used and continuously improves Score = 4	Remarks
	1.7	Are working procedures going through routine updates?					
	1.8	Are working procedures with pictures, drawing and videos?					
	1.9	Are knowledge materials controlled by revisions?					
2. Quality systems and owners	**2.1**	**Are there daily quality updates meetings?**					
	2.2	Are there quality weekly reports weekly indicators and charts?					
	2.3	Are there full time quality owners?					
	2.4	Are there yield engineers and quality experts?					
	2.5	Are there Black belt? Green belts certified?					
	2.6	Is there SPC system in place?					
	2.7	Are there weekly reviews of SPC trend?					
	2.8	Are yield data reviewed weekly?					
	2.9	Is there internal audit system?					

(continued)

			Do not exist Score = 1	Exist but rarely used Score = 2	Exists and routinely used Score = 3	Exists routinely used and continuously improves Score = 4	Remarks
		Is there open rejects control system?					
3. Corrective actions and continues improvement	**3.1**	**Is there problem solving structured methodology as 7 steps?**					
	3.2	Is there follow up and recording of major quality events (excursions)?					
	3.3	Is there *CLCA* defined processes and reviews?					
	3.4	Is there structured operation led qualification of *NPI*?					
	3.5	Is there continues improvement of *NPI quality* and reliability throughout products generations					
	3.6	Is there supplier's quality owner?					
	3.7	Are there monthly supplier's quality reviews?					
	3.8	Are there suppliers quality indicators targets for continues improvement?					
	3.9	Is there *FMEA* expert in the operations?					

(continued)

			Do not exist Score = 1	Exist but rarely used Score = 2	Exists and routinely used Score = 3	Exists routinely used and continuously improves Score = 4	Remarks
4. Product and customer feed back	**4.1**	**Is there periodical critical parameters PPK/CPK review?**					
	4.2	Are there more than 3 critical parameters that are marginal?					
	4.3	Is there continues review of product critical parameters macro trends?					
	4.4	Is there Quality of changes review board?					
	4.5	Is there weekly/ monthly product performance at customer site data collection?					
	4.6	Are there control limits to class issues in the field?					
	4.7	Is there structured process for customer complaints resolving?					
	4.8	Is there Class/ field excursion management task force system in place?					
5. Quality culture and philosophy	**5.1**	**Are there structured quality classes in all the department curricula?**					

(continued)

			Do not exist Score = 1	Exist but rarely used Score = 2	Exists and routinely used Score = 3	Exists routinely used and continuously improves Score = 4	Remarks
	5.2	Is quality routine agenda item staffs, groups and department meetings?					
	5.3	Are operations manager leaders enrich their knowledge with classes, experts or conferences?					
	5.4	Is there benchmark of operations quality performance with other companies?					
	5.5	Is there a quality distinguished leader in the organization?					
	5.6	Are there off site meetings dedicated to quality improvement?					

38.3.2 Engineering Department Self –Assessment

			Do not exist Score = 1	Exist but rarely used Score = 2	Exists and routinely used Score = 3	Exists routinely used and continuously improves Score = 4	Remarks
1. People knowledge and experience	**1.1**	**Are the senior engineers has ten years and above of experience with the company product?**					
	1.2	Are there several engineers' recent college graduates?					

(continued)

			Do not exist Score = 1	Exist but rarely used Score = 2	Exists and routinely used Score = 3	Exists routinely used and continuously improves Score = 4	Remarks
	1.3	Are the majority of the engineering are specialists?					
	1.4	Is there an integrated cooperation between the different engineering disciplines?					
	1.5	Are there monthly and quarterly enrichment and training classes for engineers?					
	1.6	Is there internal move of engineers from and to the R&D department?					
	1.7	Are there engineers with previous experience of different technologies?					
	1.8	Does engineers visits the company customers frequently?					
2. Interface with R&D and the NPI group	**2.1**	**Does engineering NPI team is part of the R&D NPI process?**					
	2.2	Does the R&D dedicates module for the engineering department to lead their design?					
	2.3	Is *Design For Manufacturability* (*DFM*), and *Design for serviceability* (*DFS*) are integral part of the product development?					
	2.4	Are *NPI* drawings and formulations, documented from early development stage?					
	2.5	Does the company management prioritize the *PLC/PDP* (product Life					

(continued)

			Do not exist Score = 1	Exist but rarely used Score = 2	Exists and routinely used Score = 3	Exists routinely used and continuously improves Score = 4	Remarks
		Cycle/Product Development Cycle) as high priority?					
	2.6	Does Engineering department a major contributor in PLC/PDP mile stones decisions?					
	2.7	Does senior Engineers at the *NPI* group are source of information for the R&D developers?					
	2.8	Does *NPI* team improves its *KPI* from one product launch to next product launch?					
3. Process and equipment engineering group	**3.1**	**Does process engineering group improves the process *CPK* by 30–50 % after the product release to manufacturing?**					
	3.2	Does the process engineers can scale up the process by 100 % in a year?					
	3.3	Was process cost been reduced by 50 % along years?					
	3.4	Was there process reduction time?					
	3.5	Does every process engineer works with SPC and statistical analysis?					
	3.7	Does the process or equipment engineers developed patents of the company?					
	3.8	Does the group have joint projects with universities or research institute?					
4. Product engineering group	**4.1**	**Does group has weekly communication with the customers and customer services?**					

(continued)

			Do not exist Score = 1	Exist but rarely used Score = 2	Exists and routinely used Score = 3	Exists routinely used and continuously improves Score = 4	Remarks
	4.2	Does product group knows customer specific product needs and solutions?					
	4.3	Does product group defined the product process margins					
	4.4	Does product group a members in product change management and Control Change Board?					
5. Testing, laboratory and systems	**5.1**	**Does engineering department has dedicated laboratory and testing equipment?**					
	5.2	Does the lab has experts in testing methodologies and statistics?					
	5.3	Does the group has experts for testing equipment?					
	5.4	Does the engineering team owns the product configuration control and document control?					
	5.5	Does the engineering owns regulation legal and environment control?					
	5.6	Does the engineering has experts and masters in both teams?					
	5.7	Does the engineers have experts in problem solving methodologies?					
	5.8	Does the engineers have experts in FMEA methodologies?					

(continued)

		Do not exist Score = 1	Exist but rarely used Score = 2	Exists and routinely used Score = 3	Exists routinely used and continuously improves Score = 4	Remarks
5.9	Does engineering has immediate respond process for product, process or equipment deviations?					
5.10	Does engineering have task forces management experts					

38.3.3 Lean Self-Assessment

		Do not exist Score= 1	Exist but rarely exist but rarely used Score = 2	Exists and routinely exists and routinely used Score = 3	Exists routinely used and exists routinely used and continuously improves Score = 4
1	*Continuous improvement systems (including part of tools)*				
1.1	To what extend does the Organization have an embedded Continuous Improvement Culture in the workplace?				
1.2	5S—Organization is constantly progressing and used as a learning opportunity				
1.3	Kaizen Events— Organization have the knowledge and will to drive structured and task oriented improvement events				
1.4	SMED—(Single Minute Exchange of Dies)—Setup times (For all processes i.e., Administration) are constantly improved using a common and agreed view				

(continued)

		Do not exist Score= 1	Exist but rarely exist but rarely used Score = 2	Exists and routinely exists and routinely used Score = 3	Exists routinely used and exists routinely used and continuously improves Score = 4
1.5	A3—Problem Solving—Employees (at all departments) initiate learning for every non-standard event till reaching root cause elimination				
1.6	Continuous improvement initiatives are easily conducted through the organization and by all employees				
2	***Value stream processes***				
2.1	Internal processes are analyzed as two ways customer–supplier interaction				
2.2	Customer supplier connections (internal and external) are reviewed and improved in a structured way				
2.3	Value stream mapping is part of the day to day activity at all levels (based on complexity)				
2.4	First line employees are able to VSM their activities or part of them				
2.5	Flows: Information/ Material/People.... flows are defined clearly and improved In a structured way (Push/PULL)				
3	***Rules and principles***				
3.1	Operational philosophy is based on common rules and principles (i.e., waste elimination, standardization, and problem solving, learning from successes...)				

(continued)

		Do not exist Score= 1	Exist but rarely exist but rarely used Score = 2	Exists and routinely exists and routinely used Score = 3	Exists routinely used and exists routinely used and continuously improves Score = 4
3.2	Issues are addressed close to the place of occurrence (in the Gemba) rather than in the meeting rooms				
3.3	Employees at all levels and at all departments knows how to standardize activities/work				
3.4	Standardization is recognized as one of the main drivers for improvement				
3.5	Employees have a common view and knowledge about value added vs. non value added activities?				
3.6	Systematic waste elimination (7 deadly wastes) is part of the day to day way of thinking and behaving in the organization				
3.7	The organization learns from both mistakes and successes in a similar way				
4	**Breakthrough systems**				
4.1	The organization use a metrics feedback system at all levels to track and drive improvement across all parameters				
4.2	Organizational communication is used to surface problems and share learning and solutions				
4.3	Accounting systems support delivery of the right outputs to reflect contribution of LEAN activities				

(continued)

		Do not exist Score= 1	Exist but rarely exist but rarely used Score = 2	Exists and routinely exists and routinely used Score = 3	Exists routinely used and exists routinely used and continuously improves Score = 4
4.4	Continuous improvement impact is calculated and reflected throughout the whole organization				
4.5	The workplace environment support making individual and teams to become high performers				
5	**Leadership and culture**				
5.1	Top management "Walk the Talk", role model LEAN philosophy by coaching employees and empowering a learning organization				
5.2	Managers actively support LEAN implementation by commitment and action				
5.3	Management only give permission for some initiatives				
5.4	Problems are welcomed and perceived as an opportunity for improvement				
5.5	In general employees share a common language and a shared view while looking at their work or work of others				
5.6	Leaders empower employees to take ownership on their Improvements initiatives				
5.7	Leaders play an active role in training employees about the need and the way to improve their work				

(continued)

		Do not exist Score= 1	Exist but rarely exist but rarely used Score = 2	Exists and routinely exists and routinely used Score = 3	Exists routinely used and exists routinely used and continuously improves Score = 4
5.8	Resources are allocated to enhance coaching and teaching capabilities among managers				

38.3.4 People Satisfaction, Motivation and Contribution Assessment

	NA	Not at all	A little	To some extent	To a large extent	A lot
	0	1	2	3	4	5
Team work						
I am satisfied with the amount of cooperation between the factory's departments						
My team works in cooperation to get the work done						
My team works in a high level of commitment and responsibility						
The team members trust each other and are close to one another						
My team mates are willing to support me when I need help						
I feel valuable and meaningful in my team						
People management						
My manager is open to hear my suggestions/ideas						
My manager handles performance problems openly and directly						
During the year I receive regular feedback from my managers, which allows me to improve my performance						
My manager defines and sets clear personal goals and expectations						
I have a personal meetings with my direct manager once a week						

(continued)

	NA	Not at all	A little	To some extent	To a large extent	A lot
	0	1	2	3	4	5
My manager contributes to the improvement of my professional abilities by training and mentoring						
My manager works according to values of excellence and sets a personal example for me						
I receive recognition and appreciation for my achievements at work from my manager						
I feel free to present my opinions and ideas to my manager						
When I need personal help from my manager he/she is there for me						
I understand the connections between my work and the company's results						
I feel my contribution is appreciated						
I am empowered and can make decisions that influence my work						
My manager is available to me when I have questions or need help						
My manager listens to me						
I am satisfied with the way I am managed						
Transparency and communication						
I am updated about what is happening in the organization						
I am satisfied with the business information transferred to me by my manager						
I can communicate my concerns and ideas to any of the management levels above my manager						
Existing information sources allow me to stay up to date on what is happening in the organization						
I am updated in an orderly and ongoing manner of decisions and changes in my team						

(continued)

	NA	Not at all	A little	To some extent	To a large extent	A lot
	0	1	2	3	4	5
Sharing knowledge and involvement in the organization						
I can attain the information required in order to do my work						
I am adequately involved in decisions that affect my work						
I influence the streamlining and saving efforts in the organization						
The atmosphere in the team is characterized by cooperation and passing of information between the workers						
My team learns from experience, draw conclusions and improve accordingly						
Effectiveness and efficiency						
My team uses its resources effectively in order to achieve its goals						
My team works according to clear and measurable goals and objectives						
It is common to challenge the way things are usually done						
I constantly look for ways to do my work better						
In my team we work efficiently						
My teams sifts tasks and processes that are not critical						
My team looks for ways to change work processes in order to improve production						
My team uses efficient decision making processes						
My team uses efficiency and information for work management needs						
If I notice any problem at work I take the responsibility to make sure the problem is solved						

(continued)

	NA	Not at all	A little	To some extent	To a large extent	A lot
	0	1	2	3	4	5
Training and personal development						
The training I receive supplies me with the knowledge and skills required in order to do my work in the best way						
I evolve and learn new things through my work						
I have the tools and equipment required to do my work in the best way possible						
During the past 12 months I could take advantage of possibilities to strengthen my professional knowledge and improve my personal skills						
I have the authority to do my work as expected of me						
I feel self-fulfillment from my work						
My manager encourages me to fulfill my potential						
I have a personal development program in the organization						

38.4   Appendix D

There are many excellent books to learn management and best operation practices. In this chapter, we summarize and recommend some of the operation management books. We start our recommendations from the personal level, and then go to the team and the company level. On the personal level we go over practices from Covey's seven habits of highly effective people (Covey, 1996). Then on the team level we review practices from several books as Gung Ho by Blanchard and Bowels (Blanchard & Bowles, 1998). In several chapters of our book we quote the theory of constraint as an essential theory and tool for operation management, in this chapter we review the Goal by Goldratt as the basic book to learn managing operations through its philosophy (Goldratt, 1992).

As operations methodologies are dynamics and changes like every other discipline it is important to keep studying from the following books as well as from new publications in the field.

References

Blanchard, K., & Bowles, S. (1998). *Gung Ho: The creation of raving fans*. New York: William Marrow.

Boyatzis, E. R., & McKee, A. (2005). *Resonant leadership: Renewing yourself and connecting with others through mindfulness, hope, and compassion*. Boston, MA: HBS press.

Buckingham, M., & Clifton, D. O. (2001). *Now discover your strengths*. New York: Gallup Organization.

Collins, J. (2001). *Good to great: Why some companies make the leap…and others don't*. New York: Harper Business Books.

Collins, J., & Porras, J. I. (1994). *Build to last: Successful habits of visionary companies*. New York: HarperCollins Books.

Covey, S. (1996). *The seven habits of highly effective people*. Tel Aviv: Oram.

Daniels, W. R., & Mathers, J. G. (1997). *Change- ABLE organization: Key management practices for speed and flexibility*. Mill Valley, CA: ACT Publishing.

Gladwell, M. (2008). *Outliers*. Or Yehuda: Kinneret, Zmora-Bitan, Dvir.

Goldratt, E. M. (1992). *The goal: A process of ongoing improvement*. Croton-on-Hudson, NY: North River Press.

Iacocca, L., & Novac, W. (1984). *IACOCCA: An autobiography*. New York: Bantam Books.

Isaacson, W. (2012). *Steve jobs*. Ben Shemen: Modan.

Louis, V., & Gerstner, L. V. (2002). *Who says elephants can't dance? Inside IBM historic turn-around*. New York: Harper Business Books.

Lundin, S. C., Paul, H., Christensen, J., & Strand, P. (2000). *Fish! Tales: Real-life stories to help you transform your workplace and your life*. New York: Hyperion.

Acknowledgements

Prof. Adar Kalir for writing on Variability in Operations, from his many years of industrial experience and academic research leading breakthroughs in control of variability in the semiconductor production lines.

Albert Elmaleh for summarizing the world of *LEAN*, based on his vast experience in the semiconductor and biotechnology industries, and driving and implementing *LEAN* in different and various industries.

Avigail Newman for the detailed and professional editing and for the significant support in bringing the manuscript to print.

Chen Goldner for detailed review of the manuscript and valuable feedback and professional supportive and recommendations. Also for writing the chapter on Kanban logistics methodology.

David Tomer for supporting me along ten years in implementing operational excellence through jointly thinking, building and presenting our strategies in lean concepts.

Dvir Ravoy for leading numerous FMEA studies and help in the FMEA chapter writing, and for major contribution in long terms suppliers yield improvement projects, their analysis and charts (Fig. 26).

Eyal Elazar for writing the section on production material Just in Time management from his vast experience optimizing inventory through applying the JIT methodology.

Dr. Gerry Tanny for going over several chapters and adding from his pioneering working experience in transforming science to high technology industry and contributing with his rich writing.

Izhak Abisdris for describing Return on Investment practices from his experience on operations budget control and tight and effective operations cost management.

Izik Polad for supporting me in implementing advance DSS systems reviewing the DSS chapter and adding the DSS scheme.

Moshe Dvir. Many thanks to Moshe Dvir for 30 years of friendship, and knowledge sharing on operational excellence. Those years of conversations sharing Moshe Dvir extensive experiences from several companies had important contribution. Special thanks for Moshe Dvir and Michal for the hospitality while writing the book. And for writing the chapter on *ERP*.

Pho, Soon Hin. For reading in depth the manuscript and supporting with professional feed-back and for many years of operations collaboration.

Yoav Kotzer. Special thanks to Yoav Kotzer for encouraging me to write the book and more than ten years of continuous consulting solving challenges in the operations world. Also for helping in writing the chapter on Hiring for operations from his 30 years of experience with hiring.

Yaccov Gidron. For many years' of discussions and practicing together LEAN and innovation implementation in operations and for his valuable feedback while reading the book.

Yoav, Yacobovitz, for the continuous support while reviewing chapters and value remarks. Also for adding ideas from his 30 years of experience managing technology and engineers in semiconductor, biotechnology and in the chemistry industries.

For reading chapters and supporting with very valuable feedback and offering their many years of knowledge and assistance in operations, thank you to Tang Keng Hiong and Jason Kang.

Many thanks to our many friends working together at the different operations departments, contributing and developing together the exciting knowledge of operational excellence.

Printed by Printforce, the Netherlands